CHURCHMOUSE
TALES

A Children's Book for Grown-Ups

CHURCHMOUSE
TALES

Cynical Bedtime Reading

GARY MOORE

ILLUSTRATIONS BY ANNE WARWICK

CHARGING RAM BOOKS
TORONTO

To Colonel C Nelson R.A.
Who once said that I was the most illiterate army officer
that he had ever met.

He was right!

CHARGING RAM BOOKS & E-BOOKS,
an imprint of 2204112 Ontario Inc., Toronto, Canada,
may be ordered through booksellers or by contacting:

WWW.CHARGINGRAM.COM.

FEBRUARY 1, 2011

FIRST EDITION

ISBN: 978-0-9867012-6-9- softcover
ISBN: 978-0-9867012-7-6 - eBook

Library and Archives Canada – Bibliothèque et Archives Canada
www.collectionscanada.gc.ca

Table of Contents

ALBERT'S PENGUIN

It is rare to find yourself in the position of being the accidental owner of a penguin. But that was just the situation that Alfred Carsey found himself in.

He had gone to the local auction house in order to buy a dining table that he fancied, but in his eagerness to secure said dining table, had accidentally submitted a bid on a penguin instead.

As nobody else had bid (for good reason), Albert found himself driving home with a penguin sitting beside him.

Not knowing a great deal about the needs and wants of his new acquisition, Albert put the penguin in the bath and went to see if there was any fish in the fridge that he could feed it.

When he returned with a bag of frozen prawns, he found that the penguin had torn the head off of his plastic duck and was now rubbing itself down with a towel and liberally dousing itself with Albert's best aftershave. Albert went to grab the bottle, but the penguin glared at him with such malevolence that Albert stopped in his tracks.

It is well known that the glare of a penguin is something that will put the fear of God into most animals and is the reason why Lions no longer populate the Antarctic.

Albert slowly backed out of the bathroom, leaving the creature to finish its ablutions.

Albert made himself a cup of tea and retired to the lounge to think what to do. He decided that the problem could wait until the morning and so he settled himself down in front of the TV. He had just become absorbed in a particularly interesting programme about bus shelters when the penguin sauntered into the room, sat down beside him, picked up the remote control and changed the TV to the Fish n' Violence channel.

Albert edged off his seat and quietly crept up to bed, locking the bedroom door behind him.

The next morning Albert set off to his work at the local lolly stick factory. He had not slept well and was glad to see that the penguin was fast asleep on the sofa amidst a litter of beer cans and empty crisp packets. It was snoring loudly and Albert thought it wise to let sleeping penguins lie.

When he returned that evening, the penguin was waiting for him. It snatched Albert's bag of groceries from him and tipped the contents onto the floor before selecting a packet of chocolate bars and a tub of ice cream, waddling off in the direction of the bedroom.

Albert looked around and saw that the mess made by the penguin the previous night had not been cleared up, but had been added to. The place was an absolute tip! What was the point of having a penguin if it just meant more work and more expenditure? He didn't want to pass the evening watching the Fish n' Violence channel again while his erstwhile pet ate him out of house and home, and so he went to the pub.

While he was there, he got into conversation with the pub landlord. Mr. McVitie had been in the pub trade a long time and could tell when a customer had come in to drown his sorrows.

"Penguin trouble is it?" he asked.

"How could you tell?" replied Albert.

"See it all the time. In the house on its own is it?"

Albert nodded and took a pull of his beer. Mr. McVitie leaned forward and said in a quiet voice:

"What you need to do is get it another penguin to keep it company. That normally keeps them happy. Takes their mind off things you see."

When Albert got home from the pub slightly the worse for wear, the first thing he saw when he opened the door was the penguin standing before him with its arms folded across its chest, tapping its foot on the floor and with a "And what time do you call this?" expression on its face.

Albert tried to ignore it and went straight up to his bed.

The next day Albert thought about what Mr. McVitie had said. It seemed to make sense and on the way home, he called in at the pub to see if the landlord knew of anyone who was selling a spare penguin.

As luck would have it, it appeared that Mr. McVitie himself had a penguin that he was prepared to sell at a reasonable fee. "How fortuitous," thought Albert.

Mr. McVitie seemed quite pleased as well.

Far from bringing calm into the house, the addition of a second penguin simply doubled the level of discomfort. Not only were they hogging the TV remote control, but they would stay up all night playing loud music and damaging the furniture. They would tut over the food that Albert gave them and sneer at his cd collection. After a week, they made it clear to Albert that the bath was not big enough for two penguins and that he should be thinking of providing them with a pool.

On reflection, Albert realised that this was not a bad idea. If he built a pool in his back yard, the penguins would spend most of their time there and Albert would get his remote control back. He got out his toolbox and set to with a vengeance.

By the following Sunday the pool was ready and when the penguins had shuffled out of the back door, Albert slammed it behind them and nailed it shut.

That night having thrown some fish out of his back bedroom window to the penguins to stop them hammering on the door, he settled down to the first quiet night he'd had in weeks.

Word soon got round that Albert had a penguin pool in his back yard and over the next month the number of penguins increased as people threw their own troublesome penguins over Albert's back wall. At one time he thought that he had glimpsed old Mrs. Cooper from the post office loitering nearby with a suspiciously penguin-shaped bundle under her arm, waiting for a moment when he was not looking.

In a very short space of time, there was hardly a blade of grass in Albert's back yard that didn't have a penguin sitting on it. Things were rapidly getting out of hand and something needed to be done.

One thing that Albert had learned while living with penguins was that they are crazy about fish. I mean, you might like a nice piece of poached haddock for your dinner now and again, but penguins will kill for something scaly with gills. They will eat as much as they can get hold of and the only way to keep them calm is to constantly throw wet fish at them. So Albert borrowed his brother's van and one night laid a trail of sardines from the back yard into the back of it. The penguins followed the trail and when they were all inside, Albert closed the back doors and drove into the city. He parked opposite the aquarium and when he reopened the doors, all of the penguins rushed out and headed for the main entrance.

Before they had realised that the aquarium was closed for the night, Albert was gone.

It was natural that a large gang of homeless penguins in a strange city should drift into the sort of employment that best suited their characters. As they are neither literate, numerate nor great orators, it was no surprise to find that they went into security work.

So when you are preparing to go out to a night club and want to be sure of getting past the penguin guarding the door when you get there, don't forget to put a pilchard in your pocket.

***

Brenda's Magnificent Creation

©Anne Warwick 2011

Brenda Dubbins lived a quiet sedentary life in a small unremarkable town. She was a woman of simple needs. She looked after the house, did the shopping and occasionally knitted the odd thing for her grandchildren.

If she had a passion, it was for flowers. She would spend hours pottering about in the garden, pulling weeds from the flower beds and tidying things up. She grew plants from seed and also from cuttings. Her greatest desire was to one day win first prize at the annual flower show. Over the years, her displays of flowers had steadily climbed the rankings of the local cultivators, resulting in the giddy heights of 3rd place a few years ago.

The next flower show was due to be held in less than 2 months time and this year Brenda thought that she had a good chance of winning the best in show prize. This was due to a hybrid flower that she had been working on. At the moment it was no more than a small green shoot with the flower barely visible, but she could see that this little plant had the potential to become something special.

She lavished attention on it and over the next week or so the flower began to bloom.

It is difficult to express in words, the magnificence of Brenda's flower. It had an elegant vivid green stem and its lush petals were a veritable kaleidoscope of colour from soft pale pinks, through cornflower blue, to deep scarlet reds. Every colour and shade of the spectrum was to be found in Brenda's creation. It was like tasting champagne with your eyes.

Brenda went to find her husband Ted, in order to show him what she had produced.

Mr. Dubbins had been gently dozing in front of the television when his wife shook him by the shoulder and woke him up. He put his slippers on and shuffled along behind her to the potting shed in order to see what she was so worked up about.

When they arrived, all he could see was a small wooden table that had been placed in the centre of the floor. Upon the table was something about the size of a can of soda with a cloth covering it.

Brenda stood behind the table, her eyes shining, her face flushed and her chest heaving up and down. Ted had not seen her so excited since that evening last year when he had found the jar of honey in the bedside cabinet after they had finished off the bottle of sherry that next door had given them for Christmas.

Brenda took the cloth in between her thumb and forefinger, and with a loud cry of "Da-Dah" whipped away the cloth to reveal the flower.

"What do you think?" She asked.

Ted Dubbins stood and looked at the stunningly beautiful multi-coloured plant before him.

"It's wonderful" he said.

He took two steps towards it and bent down to sniff its perfume.

The scent hit him in much the same way that a howitzer shell hits a dog kennel. The small beautiful little plant in front of him was giving off the rank odour of a decomposing badger. It was like having a dozen angry hornets shoved up your nose! Ted Dubbins staggered back as though he had been hit with a baseball bat.

"My God! That stinks to high heaven," he exclaimed.

Brenda looked shocked. She had noticed the smell before, but had thought that it was the drains or that next door's tom cat had got in again. She put the cloth back over the flower and went to make her husband a cup of tea.

Over the next few days, Brenda thought about what she could do regarding the horrible stench that emanated from the flower. She decided to plant it in the garden where hopefully with more air around it, the thing would not be so pungent.

Unfortunately, as the flower grew, the smell from it became worse and worse. In order to contain the smell, Brenda retrieved an old fish tank from the loft and placed it upside down over the flower.

The decomposing badger smell still wafted out from time to time, but it improved things a little.

A week later Brenda invited Mrs. Frobisher, the president of the local gardening society around on the pretence of wanting to give her some newly knitted baby clothes for her niece.

Brenda made sure that when Mrs. Frobisher arrived, she was served tea and cake by the window that overlooked the garden. In the course of the conversation, she casually mentioned that she was thinking of entering a new type of flower into the forthcoming flower show and pointed out the inverted fish tank to her guest. Mrs.

Frobisher was visibly impressed by what she saw through Brenda's window and asked to go and examine the plant more closely. Brenda only just prevented her from entering the garden by saying that Ted was in the habit of sunbathing nude round about this time and it would be embarrassing if they stumbled across him.

The problem with covering the flower with a glass fish tank was that within the warm rarefied atmosphere, the flower thrived and grew at a prestigious rate. Brenda was soon forced to replace the tank with a bigger one. While she was changing the tanks over, the smell, which had become noticeably worse, obliged her to wear a snorkelling mask and wrap a sock around her mouth.

The flower continued to grow, and as it expanded, it soon lifted the new bigger tank off of the ground with the result that overflying birds fell out of the sky.

Ted was sent down to the garden centre to buy a greenhouse to erect around it.

The problem of the smell was finally solved by a relatively simple cure. During a visit to Mrs. Frobisher's house for cocktails one night, Brenda noticed that Mrs. Frobisher kept a box of matches and an ashtray in her toilet. Knowing that Mrs. Frobisher didn't smoke, this seemed to be a curious thing and she mentioned it to her husband when they got home.

Ted, who knew more things than he normally let on to, explained to his wife that the reason for the matches was that after completing one's toiletry needs, the lighting of a match would burn off any noxious gasses in the toilet, leaving the way clear for the next user.

This was the smartest thing that Brenda had ever heard her husband say in nearly forty years of marriage. If the lighting of a match could clear the smell from Mrs. Frobisher's toilet, then the same principle could be applied to the greenhouse in the garden.

The following morning, Brenda dressed her husband in a diving suit and despatched him together with a large candle and a new box of matches to the greenhouse. The flower, with its brilliant array of colours and hues, was now nearly eight feet high and Mr. Dubbins viewed it through the glass with a mixture of awe and hatred in roughly equal measure. Prudently, he decided to light the candle before entering. However, upon opening the door, within the space of a few seconds, the greenhouse gasses ignited, with the result that Ted was blown onto his back and all of the panes of glass in the greenhouse shattered.

Fortunately, he managed to keep hold of the candle and when he looked at it, saw that it was burning like a blowtorch. The theory worked!

Brenda was delighted. She knew that she could now display her flower at the show without people throwing up or fainting whenever they got within 10 yards of it. She would surely win first prize.

After all her years of hard work victory would finally be hers.

After attending to her husband's wounds, she sent him down to the garden centre to buy a six foot wide plant pot, a box of candles and a portable greenhouse.

***

SecuriCat

Eric Morris had 127 hamsters and unfortunately each and every one of them was colour blind, which was a shame as he had been training them up to be electricians.

You see, Eric spent his days fixing computers for other people, and one day, he had the bright idea that rather than going to the trouble of taking the thing apart to mend it, he could just pop a trained hamster inside and it would fix the computer for him.

As a result he spent a lot of time and effort training his animals in all respects of computer maintenance. Lectures had been set, flow charts produced and examinations taken.

After two weeks, his hamsters understood how all of the switches and cogs and springs and bits of plastic went together, and also what all the various bits and pieces did. But whenever Eric put one of his hamsters into a computer, a red wire would be put where a blue wire should go and — Pow! — another computer would explode.

Eric would be left with a box of junk to dispose of and a smouldering rodent to bandage up.

And so Eric found that he was stuck with 127 highly skilled, but slightly damaged hamsters that he had no use for.

He decided to call in at the local computer factory,

to see if they could make use of them.

Granny Smith, the hard-nosed owner of Fruit Technical Products Inc., was not particularly keen on animals. Anything without flashing lights and a USB lead hanging out of the back of it held no interest for her. But once Eric had demonstrated his hamsters in front of her, she saw a golden business opportunity.

She bought 50 of the hamsters from Eric and sent them off to the night watchman to train as industrial spies.

She figured that the hamsters could be infiltrated into the premises of her arch rival — The Raincoat Computer Co. down the road. With their technical knowledge, the hamsters could bring back information about the new products that her competitor was developing. It may even be possible, she thought, to sack the staff of her own research and development department and save some money. All they seemed to do down there all day was goof around and throw paper balls at each other anyway.

The hamsters were duly briefed and released into the premises of the unsuspecting Raincoat Computer Co. They immediately scurried about, making notes and memorising circuit boards.

Results happened quickly. Granny Smith was now able to launch new products ahead of her rivals.

Sales went up, and profits soared.

Eric Morris still had 77 hamsters left in his house. Granny Smith had been too mean to buy more than 50 and he wondered what to do with the rest. He realized that if one computer firm would buy hamsters from him, then it might be possible to sell the rest to another.

The following morning, he visited the Raincoat Computer Co and had a meeting with the board of directors.

The management at raincoat had been wondering why their sales had gone down sharply and how it was that Granny Smith had been able to launch products that were strikingly similar to the ones they had been developing. They had not connected the recent influx of hamsters running around their factory with their poor trading performance until Eric pointed out what had been happening.

"Well," said the Managing Director, "If Granny Smith can use them, so can we." Raincoat bought all of Eric's remaining stock.

Within a short time, parity between the rival firms had been reached. The only difference being, that both companies now had additional expenditure for hamster wheels and bags of nuts.

Back at Fruit Technology, Granny Smith noticed that sales and profits had returned to their pre-hamster level. She had also noticed that there seemed to be a lot of hamsters running around her factory and that she didn't recognise most of them. It dawned on her that her pre-emptive hamster strike on her rival had been reciprocated. She had lost her commercial advantage and so would have to find a way to get rid of her competitor's furry spies. She pulled the yellow pages from her desk drawer and ran her finger down the list of companies that it showed. Her finger stopped at one particular advert. It read:
SECURICAT. ALL YOUR FELINE SECURITY

NEEDS ANSWERED.

She picked up the phone and dialled the number.

Securicat was run by cats for cats. They would work for whoever paid them the most. As any cat owner will tell you, loyalty and morals are not their strong points. They were ruthless and professional and could show testimonials from the local farmer, and the man who ran the grain store near the railway.

They drove a hard bargain with Granny Smith. Sure, they would rid her of the hamster problem, but it would cost more than the usual saucer of milk. They wanted balls of wool as well!

Granny Smith looked in her purse and reluctantly agreed.

The cats set to their task with a vengeance. Unsuspecting hamsters found that instead of working their way through a computer, they were working their way through the digestive system of a cat instead. Two weeks after the carnage had begun, the factory was hamster free. Granny Smith was delighted at the results and promptly sacked all of the cats.

With the supply of milk and balls of wool now denied to them, the cats moved down the road and offered their services to Raincoat Computers. They were taken on and within two weeks had achieved the same results as before.

When they had finished, they were sacked from there as well.

Now cats ain't stupid. They may not know much about computers or tax breaks or profit forecasts, but they are not dumb. They realized that, by ridding the two factories of their rodent problems, they had done themselves out of a job. And saucers of milk don't grow on trees you know.

One night they hatched a plan.

They went out and stole twenty new hamsters from the local pet shop, and released them into both computer factories. These hamsters were not electrical engineers, but that didn't matter. Both companies had lost their trained hamsters and assumed that the ones running around their factories belonged to their rivals.

Phone books were brought out and frantic calls made to Securicat.

This time the cats had a better idea of their value. They demanded not only milk and balls of wool, but fish as well! The companies had no choice. They were terrified of losing their trade secrets and so paid the cats what they asked for.

Securicat moved its extermination squads back into the factories. This time though, they didn't kill the hamsters. Instead they made sure that the hamsters remained visible. They knew that visible hamsters mean constant fish.

When the cats were questioned as to why it was taking so long to get rid of the vermin, they would say:

"These are different hamsters," which was true.

"They are smarter than the last lot," which was false.

"It's going to take more time. We think that we can control them, but not eradicate them totally," which was true and false.

Things went on in this fashion for some time. But as the

weeks passed, the company accountants became restless. Fish isn't cheap and the cost of buying so much cut deeply into profits.

Granny Smith decided to call in an outside consultant to look at the problem.

So it was that Eric Morris revisited the company that had first bought from him 50 highly skilled colour blind hamsters.

Using a broom and a plastic bucket, Eric caught one of the hamsters that was running around the factory and brought it to Granny Smith's office for questioning. It soon became apparent that the hamster, while knowledgeable about nuts, did not know the first thing about computers. A second hamster was captured and under interrogation revealed the scam that the cats had been perpetrating.

When told the news, Granny Smith bolted upright in her chair. She had suspected that the cats were up to something for some time as there had been no decrease in the number of hamsters running around her factory. There were also balls of wool and fish bones all over the place and her furniture had been scratched as well. Something had to be done.

She took out the phone book and looked up the number of Securidog.

***

The Fall Of the Egyptian Empire

*E*gypt could and should have ruled the world.

It was once the world's most technologically advanced nation, but managed to blow it all in a most spectacular fashion. In order to understand what happened, we have to go back to the time of the Pharaohs. At that period, Egypt had a lot going for it. Nice weather, good beaches and as much curried goat as you could possibly eat. The Egyptians themselves had invented many useful things including flower pots, hats and fondue sets. Only the spectre of the Ancient Greeks with their stunning technically advanced design of step ladder clouded the horizon.

In order to keep Egypt ahead of the game, the "Royal Inspectorate" would roam the known world seeking out innovation and invention wherever it was to be found and bringing the information back to the homeland, where it could be used for the benefit of the people.

One of the new inventions that they came across was on the land of a Tunisian farmer by the name of

Gubos. He had constructed a large funnel shaped structure, built of stone and open to the sky.

This structure had been filled with water that his slaves had hauled from a river some half mile distant. Gubos explained to the visiting Egyptian that as the top was larger than the bottom, it not only collected water efficiently whenever it rained, but it also gave a great weight and therefore great pressure of water at the bottom. By removing various small wooden stoppers at the bottom of his water tank, he could direct a stream of water over a considerable distance to irrigate his land. As a result, he had been able to turn arid desert into fertile soil and grew a large amount of grapes, which he turned into wine and then sold on to passing merchants. What's more, because he could control the amount of irrigation, his grapes and therefore his wine was of very high standard.

When the Royal Inspector bought this information, together with a sample of the Tunisian wines back to Egypt it aroused considerable interest. Cleopatra herself, who was known to like nothing more than a quiet night in getting sloshed with her mates, was particularly keen. If it could be put into use, the new technology could increase the annual agricultural yield significantly, with benefits in quality as well as quantity.

The inspector who had first come across the Tunisian water tank was told to submit plans to the nation's Master builders in order that half a dozen huge water tanks be constructed close to the Nile.

If the Egyptians had an Achilles heel it was the written word. At the time hieroglyphics were the normal method of recording and distributing information, and they are notoriously vague and inaccurate. The famous ancient slate of Alamain bears this out. For many years it was thought that the Alamain slate with its hieroglyphics was a shopping list and only recently has it been proved that it is actually a poem about socks. So it was that when the master builders received the plans, there was some confusion over some of the technical aspects. In particular, which way up, the plans were supposed to be. As a huge structure that was not only open to the elements, but with its foundations so small in relation to the rest of the building as to make it inherently unstable, it is no surprise to learn that the water holders or pyramids, as they were called in Egyptian, were built upside down. Had Cleopatra been sober enough to remember what they were supposed to look like, the work would probably have been stopped half-way into the project. As it was, the pyramids took so long to build that by the time they were finished, everyone had forgotten why they had been built in the first place. The cost of the project had also been so high, that on completion, the Kingdom of Egypt was effectively bankrupt. The only people who had any money were the owners of the large building firms who bought the structures back at knock down prices to use as storage, offices, publicity sites, and even family tombs. The body of Billy Tutankhamen of Tutankhamen Bros Builders was discovered interred in one some years later.

Should you be passing a holiday in Egypt, visit the ancient inverted water towers and remember that for all of their magnificence, the pyramids are what bought Ancient Egypt to its knees.

***

Mr. Letterman's Volcano

Mr. Letterman was as smug as a Cheshire cat during national Smugness week. For he was the proud owner of a volcano. Not a particularly big volcano you understand, in fact as volcanoes go, his was a touch on the small side, measuring no more than two foot high, but all the same, he had one and his neighbours didn't. So he was very pleased with himself.

Mr. Letterman's volcano stood in his back garden between the apple tree and the herbaceous border. Normally sometime during the middle of the afternoon it would give a little cough, and then belch forth a bright orange flame that would last for an hour or so before subsiding.

In order to make use of his volcano Mr. Letterman had built a barbecue over the top of it, and during fine summer days he and his wife would sit in the garden and eat al fresco under the shade of the tree.

One day, the Lettermans decided to have a barbecue. They also decided to invite Mr. Letterman's boss from the office and Mrs. Letterman's friend Doris from the fish shop on High street. They figured that it would be a good opportunity to show off the volcano in their garden.

Mrs. Letterman bought bread rolls, salad and various bits of reconstituted dead animal from the butchers to cook and Mr. Letterman busied himself with the preparation. He laid out the meat on the barbecue grill and stood next to it waving away the flies while he waited for the volcano to ignite. It seemed to be taking longer than usual to start up, so he found a stick and prodded it down the top of the thing.

Nothing happened and so he prodded it a bit harder.

There was a low rumbling sound, much like the noise made by Uncle John when he's asleep in front of the TV on Sunday afternoons. A few sparks and a wisp of smoke appeared and Mr. Letterman gave it another poke for luck. The noise steadily became louder and louder until with a sound like a clap of thunder, the volcano erupted in a shower of flame and molten lava.

The ensuing flame reached a good twenty feet in height and the force of it scattered marinated chicken legs and honey glazed pork chops all over the garden.

Mr. Letterman stood back in some alarm. His volcano had never done that before. He tried to extinguish the flames with the water from the paddling pool using a sand-castle bucket, but such was the heat, every bucket of water he threw at it instantly turned to steam and the ironed creases of his shorts fell out.

Mrs. Letterman had seen the eruption of the volcano and the disappearance of her husband in a cloud of steam through her kitchen window and went to find the yellow pages. She looked up the section that listed emergency volcano engineers and was heartened to find that one lived only a few streets away. Not only that, it appeared that he also did calls at the weekend. She dialled the number and got through to Mr. Rennie of Rennie's Volcano Breakdown Services Ltd.

A short while later Mr. Rennie pulled up in his van outside of the Letterman household and wandered around to the back garden.

"Thank goodness you've come," said a steaming Mr. Letterman, emerging from the cloud of smoke, ash and water vapour that had enveloped him.

"Oh please do something quickly," added Mrs. Letterman. "Doris is due to arrive at three."

Mr. Rennie scratched the back of his head with a carbonated sausage and surveyed the scene.

"Hmmm," he said after a while. "I think we will need a number 4 volcano plug. I'll see if I've got one in the back of the van."

Mr. Rennie went back to his van and started rummaging about among all of the volcano-related tools and materials in the back. After a while he emerged with what appeared to be a large rock.

He slowly staggered back to the volcano with the large rock and dropped it onto the top of it. He stood back and surveyed his work.

Apparently satisfied, he then presented the Lettermans with a large bill (double time at weekends) before getting back into his van and driving away.

Mr. Letterman rubbed the sweat away from where his eyebrows had once been and inspected the repair that had been made to his volcano. The rock that Mr. Rennie had put over it was not an exact fit and there were still some small flames escaping through the gaps around the edge of it. He realised that it was still not too late to save the afternoon's festivities under the charred apple tree.

Mrs. Letterman was dispatched to the supermarket

to buy more meat while he collected up the scattered pieces of the barbecue and reassembled it over the volcano.

There was not much time to go before the guests arrived and the small escaping flames would take forever to cook the meat, so he found a stick and quietly started prodding away at the gap at the edge of the rock.

A slow rumbling noise started.

***

Madame Pomerie

and the

CORPORAL

The village of Westouter in Belgium is typical of most places of its size. It has a post office, a baker's shop and a small bar and not much else. There are no attractions either natural or man-made to tempt the visitor to stay. It is a one street place where nothing much has happened for the last century. The last event of any great note was the billeting on the population of 150 British soldiers who operated a supply dump on the outskirts of the village during the First World War.

The smooth running of the village during wartime was jointly overseen by the mayor, Monsignor Andre Broue, and The British Billeting Officer, a Captain by the name of Francis Dade. M. Broue and Capt. Dade worked well together, possibly helped by the mayor's excellent grasp of English.

This enabled any misunderstandings to be quickly dealt with.

By the summer of 1917 Westouter was not a bad place to pass the war. It was far enough from the front line to be relatively safe with only the occasional stray shell from a long range gun to disturb the peace. The men worked what was practically a nine-to-five job and the food from the field kitchen, while not varied, was at least hot and regularly available.

Some of the soldiers were billeted in private houses while most were found accommodation in barns and storehouses. Capt. Dade ensured that a fair price was paid and M. Broue ensured that claims for compensation from the local residents were kept at an acceptable level.

At the end of each day, the two men would sit in Capt. Dade's small office situated in the front room of an abandoned cottage and pass the evening discussing the day's events over a glass of whisky.

One morning Capt. Dade was awoken from his slumbers by someone hammering loudly at the front door. He rose from his bed, pulled a greatcoat over his pyjamas and went to see who it was. Upon opening the door he was confronted by Mme. Pomerie, a middle aged widow of generous proportions who was the proprietress of the village *estaminet* or bar. She appeared to be highly agitated and rushed past the Captain into his office. Capt. Dade, who was not used to women rushing into his office before breakfast, at first had the ridiculous thought that he was improperly dressed and looked around for his hat before following Mme. Pomerie into the room. He barely had enough time to sit behind his desk before Madame launched into a vigorous diatribe against the British, her neighbours, the war and soldiers in general, at the end of which she announced that the estaminet would now be closed until further notice before marching back out of the door. While poor Capt. Dade had understood some of what madame had said, she had spoken so fast and with such fury that he had not caught all of it, and so when M. Broue showed up an hour later, the Captain asked if he would visit Mme. Pomerie to establish exactly what was wrong.

When M. Broue returned some time later, he brought bad news back with him. Mme. Pomerie alleged that one of her most regular customers, a good looking young soldier who was the sanitary corporal, had committed a crime against her person of a most serious nature.

The corporal, whose duties, while neither heroic nor spectacular, were nevertheless important, would normally attend to his work diligently each morning. By lunchtime, he would have finished and would spend as much of the rest of the day as money and madame would allow sipping "caffee avec" — coffee with brandy — in the estaminet. It appeared that the day before, he had been able to afford more of this mixture than usual and emboldened with drink, had, or at least had attempted, to ravish Madame. He had so far forgot himself and the respect due to a lady that he had embarked on this course without those preliminary attentions of flirting and suggestions that would have given her some warning of what his intentions were. She was naturally outraged that such a thing should happen within a year of her late husband's tragic meeting with a 5.9 inch shell just outside of Verdun which had left both parties spread over a considerable distance. Both her honour and the respect for her late husband had been violated.

By lunchtime the scandal had gone around the village like wildfire and Capt. Dade had a dilemma on his hands. Military law was quite definite as to the punishment given out to soldiers guilty of such a crime against civilian allies. A court martial would have to take place, bringing with it much unwanted attention from higher command. Capt. Dade suggested that if M. Broue could explain to Madame that the man had been drunk at the time, then perhaps the matter could be dealt with in-house.

Monsieur Broue was horrified at the suggestion. "It would be the worst possible course of action," he said. Far better to let Monsieur Broue himself go to see the injured party in order to talk to her and try to resolve the scandal.

That evening, M. Broue called at the shuttered estiminet and met with Madame Pomerie in the back parlour. They sat and talked of many things; about the Billeting officer, about the two girls who helped madame serve the drinks and cooked the omelettes that her customers bought, and the rumour that Canadian soldiers would be once again billeted in the village, which would mean more money going into madame's till. Slowly M. Broue guided the conversation around to the events of the previous night. "Poor Madame Pomerie," he said! "What an appalling thing to happen to a woman of her character and high standing." He mentioned how shocked all of the neighbours had been, particularly the women (although many had said they were not surprised and had seen it coming). Such a terrible thing must be punished of course. The honour of a Belgian woman is a sacred thing.

And these things cannot be taken lightly. Although it is a pity that such a young, gallant fellow should die before a firing squad, for Monsieur had studied British military law and knew that the penalty for such things would be death.

At this revelation, madame softened her stance a little and asked if not a lesser punishment could be handed out, for although she had been wronged, she was not a vindictive woman. "Alas no," said M. Broue, for he was somewhat of an expert on British Military law and was often called upon to advise the British themselves on matters of punishment. He was quite sure of the point. He also seemed to know a great deal about the sanitary corporal. That the man was the only child of his widowed mother. A God-fearing woman wracked with rheumatism whose only income was from cleaning the local church. She would obviously be heart-broken to hear of his execution. And after her son had been posted to Westouter as a reward for the time he had bayoneted four, or was it five Germans, single-handedly to save his unit from being over-run. Madame had no idea that he had been such a hero. She had thought that he had spent the whole of his military career in the safe duties of sanitation — which indeed he had. She did not want to see the man killed, but still could see no other alternative than to allow Military justice to take its course.

It was at this stage that M. Broue played his trump card. "The incident was all most regrettable," he said, "but there was something to be said for the corporal's good taste. After-all Madame was known far and wide for her good looks and sweet nature. Who could be surprised that this gallant, brave, fearless young man should become so smitten with her? Not for him the attractions of the two young serving girls. Those bold hussies who tempted the men with their coarse language and flirty ways; he had taken no notice of them. Had it not been that a few months ago, the corporal had informed him in strict confidence that he had fallen in love with the beautiful proprietress of the estiminet upon first setting eyes on her. That of course was why he spent so much time there.

Obviously his deep passion for her had built up until his need for her had so overwhelmed his senses that he had temporally lost control of his reason. So sad that one so young, so brave, so good looking should have to die like a dog, because of the beauty of a woman, but *"c'est la guerre."*

Madame's honour must be vindicated.

The next day the estiminet re-opened as usual and did a busy trade with many local people, who had not frequented it before, calling in to buy a small black coffee and swop some gossip. Madam Pomerie and the serving girls were there, but the corporal was not. He was under local arrest in the barn that served as his billet.

Some weeks later, Capt. Dade signed the official form submitted by a local householder allotting a certain room in a certain estiminet to a certain sanitary corporal.

***

Frog-a-Rama

Should you be at a loose end one day and looking for something to take away the joyless tedium of modern day living, why not take a trip down to Frog-a-Rama, Littlehampton's most popular nature reserve. There, you can pass an entertaining afternoon dressed in wet weather clothing pushing frogs out of trees with a long stick. This exciting pastime has been in operation for a few years now, but the story of how it came to be is a curious one.

It all started when a colony of dancing tree frogs was discovered by Beryl Harris, a keen member of many wildlife preservation societies. Up until that point it was thought that the Littlehampton dancing tree frog was extinct.

Beryl had been spending some time in the middle of Littlehampton woods studying fox droppings, when it had suddenly started to rain. She took shelter under a tree and ten minutes later was surprised to feel the unmistakable sensation of a frog falling on her head. She looked up and saw that the branch of the tree she was sheltering under was infested with dancing frogs.

The overwhelming sense of joy she felt as she was battered by falling frogs can easily be imagined.

Beryl, together with other members of the local wildlife society, made a study of the frogs. It was found that the frogs fed on insects that were foolish enough to walk, crawl or fly past them, much like normal non-tree dwelling frogs. The colony that Beryl had discovered inhabited two adjacent trees. All of the female frogs lived in one tree, where they spent their time discussing the merits of different male frogs, while all of the male frogs lived in the tree next door where they spent their time talking about football and motorbikes. During dry periods, the two separate genders kept apart, but when it rained the patter of raindrops caused all of the frogs to become agitated. They would then begin to leap up and down in a frenzied amphibian dance.

As the branches of the trees became wetter and more slippery, the occasional frog would miss its footing on the descending part of its leap and fall out of the tree. The unlucky ones hitting a few more branches on the way down.

Once on the woodland floor, there would be an opportunity for both genders to meet with the production of tadpoles being the result. A short film was made of the spectacle and broadcast at 4 a.m. one Wednesday morning a few years ago. You may have seen it.

The study of the dancing tree frogs had been going for a year and a half when the great drought of 2004 started. This was bad news for frog watchers and amorous frogs alike. No rain meant no dancing, which meant no plummeting to the ground, which meant no tadpoles. As the drought went on, the watchers became more and more concerned. If it didn't rain soon, the frogs were in danger of disappearing forever. Beryl and her wildlife group decided to do something about it. It was obvious that a way had to be found to water the frogs, but as they all lived in trees twenty feet off the ground, miles away from any mains water supply, it was not going to be easy to find a solution. The only semi-practical suggestion anyone could come up with was to use a fire engine, but there was no road into the woods for it to drive on.

As the hot dry days went on, Beryl and her group became even more concerned for the frogs welfare. By the middle of August, with the weather forecast to remain the same for some time, panic had started to set in and with no other viable alternative at hand, it was decided to hack a road through the woods to the frog colony.

Work began at once and went on 24 hours a day under the broiling sun during daylight and under huge arc lamps at night. In a monumental feat of civic engineering, the road was completed in just three days. With the asphalt barely dry, a fire engine purchased at considerable cost rolled along the road and pulled up by the trees containing the frogs. Hoses were unrolled, valves turned on and gallons of water were pumped into the air above the frogs' habitat. A great cheer went up from the small crowd of road workers and naturalists.

Unfortunately, instead of dancing, all of the frogs remained stationary. After fifteen minutes, it became apparent that they were not going to move. Beryl directed the men who were spraying the water to direct the jet onto the frogs in order to encourage them to leave the trees. Although this had the effect of getting the frogs onto the floor, as soon as they hit the ground they scurried behind the tree trunks and hid from the water. There was good reason for this. If you cast your mind back to the last time you were knocked out of a tree by water cannon, you will recall that romance was the last thing on your mind when you hit the floor. It was the same for the frogs.

After half an hour, the fire engine had run out of water and seizing their chance, all of the frogs climbed back into the trees. A second attempt was made later in the day with the same result.

What had not been realized at the time was that Littlehampton's tree frogs danced due to a partial diet of the extremely rare West Sussex wood ant. This particular ant carried an acid in its body, which when ingested caused the frogs to leap up and down when they came into contact with water.

As the ant hills that supplied the frogs with this supplement to their diet had been buried under 8 inches of tarmac when the road had been laid, it was unsurprising that the frogs no longer danced; although this fact was not known at the time.

Beryl and her group were faced with a problem. They realised that they could not blow the frogs out of the trees with hoses, but would have to direct a fine spray overhead to simulate rain and as the frogs inexplicably refused to dance, they would have to be gently helped on their way. The best way to achieve this was by using a long stick with a soft tennis ball on the end to push the frogs off the branches.

Now fire engines and tennis balls cost a lot of money, so it was decided to recoup the cost by opening the site up to the general public. Thus it was that Frog-a-Rama came to be.

Today you can not only push frogs out of trees while getting soaking wet in the process, but you can also buy postcards and cuddly toy frogs at the gift shop and have your photograph taken while holding a stick with a tennis ball on the end of it — all for a very reasonable fee.

Frog-a-Rama is just off the B2140 and is open all year round.

Well worth a visit.

***

Cookie Grundlers

The recent discovery of the body of Julie Bewley has once more brought to the public's attention the shady world of the cookie grundlers. The late Miss Bewley had been due to release her book on the workings of cookie grundling in two weeks time, but since she was found battered to death in an alleyway with a box of Jaffa cakes, her publishers have taken fright and pulled the book.

It is important to lay bare the facts about cookie grundling in order that there can be a full and open debate on the subject, but the level of corruption and violence that the cookie grundlers are prepared to use to keep their position, makes it unlikely that all of the facts will be available to the public.

As you probably know the black art of cookie grundling goes back many years. The first recorded instance being in 1931 at the Amalgamated biscuit works in Scarborough, when Dutch grandmother Alice Van-Rental approached the board of Amalgamated biscuits with her proposal to increase their profits by 5%, by grundling their cookie output. The board agreed and the World of baked confectionery items changed forever on that fateful day. Since then, the power and influence of the world-wide sisterhood of cookie grundlers has steadily increased.

In order to understand the full impact of what Alice Van-Rental proposed, one must realise that before 1931 uneaten cookies would go stale in a similar manner to bread, i.e., as they dried out they would harden, but by introducing grundling into the manufacturing process, cookies would become softer rather than harder once they were exposed to the air. This meant that whenever a cookie was taken from the cookie jar and dunked into a cup of coffee or a glass of milk the consumer wouldn't know for certain how long to leave it absorbing the liquid before the thing disintegrated and fell into the beverage. It is a quirk of human nature that although the consumer was happily eating sodden cookies and drinking coffee a few seconds before, once the cookie had fallen into the coffee cup, they would throw it away and start with a fresh cup of coffee and a replacement cookie even though the ingredients of their snack had remained the same. This means that for every unconsumed cookie that found its way to the bottom of the coffee mug another one would be purchased thus increasing sales.

The profits to be made from cookie manufacture are simply staggering. Forget drugs, oil, or banking. If you want to be playing with the big boys, then cookies are the way to untold fortune.

The profit margin on a packet of custard creams can be as high as 85% and combined with the back handers received from the coffee brokers, it is no wonder that biscuit manufacturers now control much of international finance. You try turning that that kind of money over with an illegal shipment of cocaine, it's impossible to achieve it. The grundlers understand this of course and they have used their unique position to lever more and more money from the big factories for themselves and in the process have become the most wealthy section of society.

Ms. Bewley had managed to infiltrate the International Sisterhood of Cookie Grundlers and had spent a month grundling cookies on the ginger nut line of one of the largest cookie manufacturers in the country before she was killed. What she had discovered was that the grundling process was nothing more than a sham. The mystical grundling stick that she used had no special powers and was merely a golf club with the end cut off and a gerbil taped onto it. Not only that, but the grundling sack, which everyone thought contained the magical powder and chants vital to the grundling process, actually contained nothing more than a packet of sandwiches, a hair brush and a woman's magazine. The act of grundling involved nothing more than Ms. Bewley locking herself into the factory and putting her feet up while reading her magazine for an hour. The actual reason why cookies go soft, rather than hard, is due to the fact that before 1931, they were made with very little fat or sugar. Both ingredients, having a certain amount of addictiveness, help to explain the growth in sales. Alice Van-Rental had approached the industry at the perfect time, just as the recipes were being changed, and nobody had thought to question her.

Ms. Bewley's information, should it find a publisher with the courage to print and distribute it, will, at a stroke, wipe out a complete craft, albeit a fake one. As cookie grundlers are the only people with more money than they know what to do with, the pressure being brought to bear by the manufacturers of luxury goods, such as gold mop buckets and diamond studded toilet roll holders, to suppress the story will be difficult to ignore.

The next journalist to break ranks will be well advised to be very wary of anyone coming towards them with a packet of shortbread in their hand.

***

THE GERMAN INVASION OF POLAND

The German Chancellor's morning was ruined by the ringing of the telephone, or rather by the information that the caller relayed into her ear.

The caller in question was the Polish foreign Minister and he informed the Chancellor that Germany had once again invaded his country despite having been told on numerous occasions that Poland didn't want to be invaded and he wanted to know what she was going to do about it.

The Chancellor closed her eyes and rubbed the bridge of her nose. She had been dreading this happening and although she had been briefed by her staff on the likelihood of it occurring at some point during her time in charge of the country, she was still not fully prepared for it. "I'm terribly sorry," she said to the understandably annoyed Polish foreign minister at the other end of the line and she went on to assure him that matters would be put right as soon as possible.

After replacing the receiver, she once more picked it up and dialled the number of the colonel in charge of the country's border guards in order to establish exactly what had taken place. He dutifully informed her that yes, unfortunately, the country had started to get up to its old tricks once more. Apparently during the previous night, the countryside had expanded and roughly 20 acres of Germany had fallen over the border and covered a similar sized part of Poland. Regrettably, the border line had not been strong enough to hold it in and the first they had known about it was when a Polish farmer called to say that his pig sty was covered by bits of Germany.

The Chancellor once more rubbed the bridge of her nose. She could sense a headache coming on and it was shaping up to be a long hard day. Not only would she have to task someone to go and shovel the expanded section of Germany back across the border, but she would also have to go on TV to give the country a good talking to, which meant that she would have to wear her "stern talking" business suit and would also have to get her hair done.

This sort of thing used to happen quite a lot to Germany. In the past, whenever the country expanded into somebody else's, they would send troops to get the land back, but what with the language problem and the unreliability of maps following the country spilling over the border onto land ruled by someone else, there would often be misunderstandings, which generally resulted in fights starting, which would then spiral out of control. Before you knew where you were, it had evolved into a full scale war.

Part of the trouble was the way that the Germans looked at the problem. As a race of efficient, methodical problem-solvers, they wanted to control the way their country acted and when it didn't do what it was told they couldn't help but try and put things right. The French on the other hand took a more relaxed view when France inadvertently invaded its neighbours (which admittedly weren't very often). When one of their mountains wandered across the border with Spain, they simply moved the sign saying "France", back a bit and allowed the French mountain to stay in Spain, reasoning that sooner or later, a Spanish mountain would meander across into France at which time they would move the sign saying "Spain", forward a bit. This of course didn't help the German Chancellor. As a German, she couldn't sit idly by while bits of Germany refused to behave.

The first thing she did was to call her secretary and tell her to make some coffee. Then she wrote a note sacking the interior minister. She would ask her secretary, when she arrived with the coffee, if she knew someone who spoke Polish and knew something about soil transportation, and if so, would then ask them if they wanted to be the new interior minister. Hopefully the new man could solve the problem without upsetting the Poles and she would have been seen to have taken decisive action. Pleased with her decision, she decided that it warranted an extra slice of chocolate cake. She felt that it was the least she deserved.

The phenomenon of nation-states violating each other's borders is not a new one of course, but it has only recently been properly understood. Professor Nicolas Docproffolopicuss of Athens University made the first detailed study in 1973 following the disappearance of a Greek Island, which drifted off and went missing for five days before returning to its original location. Once it had returned, it then refused to say where it had been and what it had been up to. There was deep suspicion that the island had got into bad company with a number of Turkish archipelagos and that they had led it astray, but the professor eventually discovered the island's diary, within which was the information in the form of a scribbled entry for the sixteenth of October reading : "They all hate me! I wish they would stop nagging and leave me alone!" that showed that the island was simply rebelling – as most things do before reaching maturity. In his published work, the Professor claims that these findings show that young countries are far more likely to storm off in a huff than older ones. Therefore somewhere like Russia, which has been around for longer than anyone can remember, are unlikely to move very far while a sharp eye has to be kept on a relatively new place like Zimbabwe. By the time you get back from a short trip to the post office to buy some stamps, your average Zimbabwean will often find that the complete nation has moved 300 miles to the left.

Back to Germany then … (if it's still where we left it). Germany is neither young nor old, being somewhere in the middle and so it is thought that its rambling across borders is the result of a mid-life crisis, and that given another hundred years or so, it will settle down and become more placid, preferring to sit by the fire with a travel book rather than going to see what's on the other side of the globe.

For now though as mid-life crises go, travelling the world has got to be less of a problem than other fixations such as hang gliding or folk dancing.

***

LITTLE ELEPHANTS

Now settle down and listen carefully, because there is something that I need to tell you. I suppose that I should've told you before, but you're old enough now to make your own decisions and it is better that you hear this from me rather than someone else.

I want to give you a couple of pieces of advice and if you heed them well, they will keep you in good stead for the rest of your life, so pay attention.

Never, ever, under any circumstances let anyone talk you into employing an elephant. There — I've said it now. You may be shocked, but it's for your own good.

No doubt you may have heard other people saying that elephants are cool or hip or groovy or whatever the current word for fashionable is, but don't believe them. There have been more lies told about elephants than anything else.

For example: You may have heard the phrase "Elephants never forget" This is not only totally untrue, but this is exactly opposite of what is actually the case. Elephants are always forgetting things.

Why do you think that they are all called Jumbo?

No ... I know that there was one called Dumbo, but that was a typing error, and it wasn't a real elephant, it was a cartoon one so it doesn't count.

They are all called Jumbo because none of them can remember each other's names, and rather than have an embarrassing encounter with another elephant that they may have gone to school with whose name they have forgotten, they all use the same one. That proves how forgetful they are. Next time that you come across an elephant, ask it what its post-code is. I can guarantee you that it would have forgotten.

Not that you are likely to meet many elephants as they are notoriously shy creatures. If you do see one, it will probably be trying to hide behind a coffee table or a standard lamp in a pathetic attempt to make itself inconspicuous.

Admittedly it is quite difficult for elephants to hide, and the big ones tend to live in the kitchen cupboards of the biggest houses as the cupboards there are bigger than the ones we have. The little ones, however — the ones that are about the size of a cat — they will normally live under your bed and cover themselves with fluff so you can't see them.

Of course all elephants are nocturnal and when you're asleep, they creep out and raid the fridge and the cupboards for food. They have an incredibly sweet tooth, which is the reason why the ice cream cone that you were saving disappeared before you could get to it.

You are probably asking yourself why little elephants would chose to live under your bed, when there are so many other places they could live; Wolverhampton for example.

Well, you may have been told at school that elephants come from warm climates. This is quite correct and is about the only true thing ever said about elephants. They do feel the cold quite badly.

Particularly on their trunks — you know how your nose feels cold in the winter — well, it is the same for elephants and with their long trunks, they would feel the cold much worse than most creatures. As your bedroom is nice and warm most of the time, it is an ideal place for them to live.

On some nights when they are feeling a bit chilly, before they set off to raid the fridge, they will occasionally steal a sock from your drawer to wear over their trunks. During the course of their nocturnal foraging, they may come across an unguarded bowl of peanuts. When this happens, they will suck the peanuts up through the sock. This is the reason why whenever you find a hole in your sock, it is always at the end and it always appears overnight fully formed.

Of course when they take the socks off, they forget where they have got them from and don't bother putting them back in your sock drawer, but just leave them lying around on the floor, which is why sometimes odd socks go missing.

This brings me to my second piece of advice for you. When you are getting dressed in the morning and can't find both socks, try looking under the bed!

***

Great Aunt Mabel's Folly

Jim Smith read the letter that had arrived at his house that morning and liked what he saw.

The letter was from a firm of solicitors advising him that he was a beneficiary of a will. This was something that had never happened to him before.

Apparently his great aunt Mabel had died and left him something that the letter described as "a piece of art." The letter requested that he contact the solicitors to arrange a day for him to receive said piece.

He could only vaguely remember his great aunt. She had lived 300 miles away and he must have been no more than 6 years old when he and his parents had last seen her. His only recollection of her was that she lived in a large old rambling house with her large rambling old husband and that she had a penchant for wearing brightly coloured hats.

He dialled the number of the solicitors and was put through to Mr. Spendit, the junior partner of Grabbit, Pinchit and Spendit Solicitors Ltd. Mr. Spendit offered his condolences for the loss of Jim's great aunt and informed him that following her husband's death, his great aunt had found comfort in the keeping of cats. So much so, that when she died, she had left all of her money to the local cats' home. However, she had not forgotten her great nephew Jim and had left him a piece of artwork in her will. Mr. Spendit didn't know what the artwork was exactly; only that it was in storage and could be delivered to Jim's house as soon as Jim specified a date. Jim asked that it be sent to him the following Thursday and Mr. Spendit said that he would make the arrangements.

The following Thursday, Jim took the day off work and waited for his heirloom to arrive.

At about half past ten, a large truck towing a large trailer pulled up outside of Jim's front door. On the large trailer was a large lumpy shaped thing covered by a large tarpaulin. The driver of the truck knocked on the door and asked Jim to sign for whatever it was that was under the tarpaulin. Once he had Jim's signature the driver pulled the tarpaulin from the object on the trailer to reveal what appeared to be a 25 ft. high stuffed cat that had been on the losing side of a fight with an equally large wolf. The driver craned the cat from the trailer onto Jim's front garden, loaded the tarpaulin into the back of the truck and with a cheery wave, drove off down the street.

Jim was somewhat perturbed by the thing that had been dumped in his front garden. He had been expecting an oil painting or perhaps a nice piece of silverware rather than a 25 ft. high study of the taxidermist's art.

He slowly walked around it looking at the thing from all angles. He wasn't completely sure what sort of animal it was supposed to be. It resembled a giant cat more than anything else, but it equally could have been a giant short-legged donkey or a giant long-legged badger. It had large vicious-looking teeth and claws, most of which were missing. It had only one eye and appeared to have lost half of its tail. The body of the thing was covered in fur that had originally been ginger grey. Where pieces had fallen off, they had been patched up with whatever had come to hand. Dotted here and there were patches of black and blue fur and even a piece that looked like it had once been part of a doormat.

Jim's wife Mary had watched the unloading of the hairy beast with undisguised horror. She was not very happy with having the horrible mangy looking thing put in her garden and when Jim returned from his inspection, she collared him about it.

"We can't have that thing in the front garden," she said. "You've got to get rid of it."

Jim was inclined to agree. He promised to do something about it at the week-end.

That night he went to bed secretly hoping that someone might steal it, but the next morning it was still there in all its malevolent moth eaten glory.

When he was at work, he phoned the municipal tip, to see if they would come and take it away for him. Unhappily, the man at the other end of the telephone informed him that there was nothing in his book of regulations to say that they could accept 25 ft. high stuffed animals; particularly ones that could not be readily identified to what species they belonged to. Jim would have to dispose of it himself.

When he came home that evening, Mary informed him that Mr. Jenkins from next door had been over complaining that the thing in their garden was blocking the light. She also said that the headmaster of the nursery school opposite had phoned to complain as it was scaring the children.

Not only that, but people had been pointing at her when she was at the supermarket. She wanted rid of the thing and she wanted rid of it now!

Jim could tell that his wife was a bit miffed and so that night he took a saw from his toolbox and began cutting up the giant stuffed cat-like creature that had despoiled his front garden. He filled up the back of his car with as much of it as it would hold and went around the town unloading the pieces into every dustbin and litter bin he could find. When he had filled up every litter bin in town he was forced to take the remainder to the next town where he filled up all of their litter bins as well. By eight o'clock in the morning, he had finished. He walked wearily to his bed and slept until lunchtime.

A week later, another letter arrived for Jim. It was from Grabbit, Pinchit and Spendit. The letter said that Messrs. Grabbit, Pinchit and Spendit were awfully sorry, but there had been a mistake. Great Aunt Mabel had actually left the bulk of her estate to Jim and the monster stuffed cat that was now distributed amongst every public litter bin for five miles, to the local cats' home. Would he be so good, they asked, as to return the giant cat effigy to them, so that they in turn could release Great Aunt Mabel's money.

***

The Good Luck Shop

Julie Nelson had not been having a good week.

Her boyfriend of two years had gone off on a "Boy's mini break" with his friends to Vegas, and before he had left, he had drained the bulk of their savings from the joint bank account without telling Julie that he was doing it. She had only realised what he had done when she checked the balance at the cash dispenser on Monday night.

By Tuesday night all of his clothes and belongings were in a pile outside of her apartment and the locks had been changed on the door.

On Wednesday she had been stopped by the police and fined for having a defective tail light and on Thursday, just to add to her misery, she had been fired from her job at the department store.

Admittedly, that had been her fault. She shouldn't have called the customer who was trying to get a refund for the cd player that her dog had chewed, a "stupid cow", but Julie had been stressed out at the time and she thought that the sacking had been a bit harsh.

With no job to go to on Friday, she went for a walk

downtown instead.

As she walked along with nowhere in particular to go to, she ran through the events of the week in her head. She would often do this if she was troubled or had a problem. She would also mentally talk to herself. The conversation that she had with herself that Friday went something like this:

Self: "OK dumb-ass, no job, no prospects, no money, no boyfriend. Pretty good going for a week huh."

Me: "Yeah right. Thanks for the encouragement."

"Well what are you going to do about it?"

"How the hell do I know! You tell me!"

"Well, you better do something quick or in a couple of months, you're gonna be without an apartment as well."

"Great, that really helps."

"Well it's not all your own fault. You've just been unlucky, that's all."

"Still doesn't help."

"What you need is a bunch of good luck to fall on you."

"Yeah right, nice if I knew where to find some."

It was then that the idea struck her. A switch somewhere in Julie's brain had made a connection and from seemingly nowhere she had a solution to her problems.

What was it that people wanted most? – They wanted to be lucky.

They wanted to win the lottery, get the partner of their dreams, get a great job, dodge illness and disease, and become famous.

She would sell luck!

She was so taken by the idea that she rushed over to

her friend's apartment to tell her.

When she arrived there, her friend Stacy was busy pressing her work uniform before going out to her shift at one of the local fast-food joints.

"Stacy, Stacy listen, I've just had a great idea."

Stacy groaned inwardly and went into the kitchen to make some coffee.

"If it's got anything to do with that asshole that you lived with for the last two years, then I'm not interested" She said.

"No, No, it's a business idea."

Stacy rolled her eyes and started rummaging in the cupboard for the sugar bowl. Julie followed her into the kitchen.

"Stacy, this one's brilliant; honestly."

"OK then Gloria Vanderbilt, hit me with it, but make it quick. I've' got to be at work in twenty minutes."

"I'm going to sell Luck. How good is that! I don't have to pay for it or buy it from anywhere and everyone wants it."

"You're nuts Julie. You haven't thought any of this out. Every week you come up with crazy stuff like this. Remember when you told me that you were going to make a fortune by running cat obedience classes. Nothing came of that did it?"

Stacy gave her friend a pitying look.

"Listen Julie, I gotta get to work. There're some cookies in that jar over there. Help yourself and pull the door behind you when you go. I'll ask my boss if he needs someone to clear tables."

Despite her friend's pessimism, Julie went ahead with her idea.

She found a small vacant shop that was wedged between a fancy goods store and a tyre shop in a rundown part of town and managed to get the owner to waive the deposit. She painted the walls a deep red and hauled her sofa, a desk and two chairs down from her apartment.

Above the door she hung a sign that read: "The Good Luck Shop".

On the first day she did not have a single customer. However, on the second day John Riley, the owner of the tyre shop called by to say hello to his new neighbour.

He asked her what she was selling. When Julie told him that she was selling luck, he shook his head and laughed. He figured that she wouldn't last a week.

Later that day when a customer complained to John about the cost of his tyres, John said jokingly that he should try next door, he might have more luck there. The man had to wait for his tyres to be fitted and so he wandered into Julie's shop to waste some time before he got his car back.

John Riley had seen the man go in and as a private joke, had given the guy a ten dollar discount when he came back for his car.

"Told you that you'd be lucky," he said.

Julie had realised that selling something as intangible as luck had an element of risk and so she didn't actually charge people anything. What she did was to hold her customer's hand, look into their eyes and then tell them that she had given them her luck. She could not say how lucky her customer would be or even when the luck would occur, only that it would surely come, and when it happened, the customer could return and give some of the luck back to Julie in the way of folding cash.

Her first payment was from the guy with the new set of tyres.

Over the next few weeks, people started to drift into the good luck shop and Julie built up a regular clientèle of old ladies whose cats had wandered off for a day or two and teenagers who needed the courage to ask someone for a date. She wasn't making a fortune, but she was getting by.

One day she had a visit from a local newspaper reporter. He had heard about the good luck shop and, as it was a quiet week, he thought that he would do a human interest story to pad the paper out a bit. The article duly appeared and the following week a few extra customers found their way to Julie's shop.

The story was picked up by a stringer and a short while later, a re-hash of the original story appeared in the inside pages of a regional weekly. The idea of somewhere that you could visit to get good luck seemed to amuse people.

A few weeks later Julie received a phone call from a television researcher. The caller worked for a programme entitled "Wonderful World." A family magazine type show hosted by the much loved TV presenter Cindy Ferling.

"Would it be possible," the researcher asked, "to come down and do a piece about Julie and her shop for the programme?"

"Would it be possible!" Wonderful World had an audience of millions and was shown nationally.

With free publicity like that, Julie would be swamped with customers. If it went well, she might even be able to franchise the good luck shop idea. It was not inconceivable that within 12 months she might be a millionaire. She agreed at once and it was arranged that Cindy Ferling and the film crew would turn up the following week.

The TV crew duly arrived and set to assembling cameras and microphones and lights both inside and outside of the small shop. Cindy Ferling, with her big hair, white teeth and professional smile went through the prepared script with Julie.

There would be a piece to camera followed by a short interview, then a shot of Cindy exiting the shop followed by a wrap up piece to camera.

Wonderful World had pre-recorded two actresses in their TV studio whom Julie had never seen. The actresses had apparently given glowing testimonials as to how lucky they had been since visiting the shop. These clips would be cut into the film later.

It was all a bit confusing to Julie, but it seemed to be going very well right up to the point where Cindy exited the shop and was hit by a passing number 92 bus.

That night, Julie called Stacy.

"Stacy, you know you said that your boss might have a job going clearing tables. Well —"

***

The Roller Skate Factory

© Anne Warwick 2011

*A*s any regular subscriber to "Roller" magazine (Roller's the name, skating's the game) will tell you, if you have a roller skate-related problem, then you need to talk to a Bulgarian.

For Bulgaria may not have much of a fishing industry and their cars may be made of the metal that you normally find wrapped around a stick of chewing gum, but for quality and price with regard to roller skates, they cannot be beaten.

Thus it was, that when The Western Skate Company realised that it was becoming uncompetitive, it naturally looked towards the land of the Bulgars.

The owners of Western had figured that if they got rid of their workforce and sold off their factory and machinery, they would have just enough money to buy a profitable Bulgarian concern. The skates could be made cheaply in Bulgaria and shipped to Western for packaging, distribution and marketing, thus making the company profitable once more.

Showing the cavalier disregard for the loyalty of their staff that is the hallmark of all good corporations, Western instructed their bank to look for a suitable acquisition.

Within a month the bank had found a business that

appeared to meet all the criteria. It was called The Hoota Roller Skate Works, and was owned by Mr. Boris Hoota and his well upholstered wife, Olga.

The board of Western studied the numbers and agreed to go ahead. They obviously needed someone to act as liaison between their new Bulgarian factory and their offices and so they sent a memo around asking if anyone in the company spoke Bulgarian.

Tom Smith was a production manager for Western. He spoke no Bulgarian and was not even sure where Bulgaria was, but he had heard the rumours that Western were going to close their old factory and he was smart enough to know that jobs in the roller skate industry were few and far between.

One of the marks of a good manager is the ability to lie convincingly and that was one thing that Tom had learnt to do well. Therefore, in order to keep his job, he informed the board of Western that not only was he willing to travel, but he was practically fluent in Bulgarian. The board were delighted to have found someone and once the paperwork for the sale of the old factory and the purchase of the new one had been finalised, Tom Smith was despatched to Bulgaria.

When he arrived at Western's new factory, he was greeted by Boris Hoota himself. Boris had agreed to stay on for three months in order to let the new man settle in.

They shook hands and Tom said "Hello."

Boris said something unintelligible in return.

The two men stood grinning at each other while each of them tried to think of a word or phrase of the other one's language. After a few minutes silence, it was apparent that communication would be a bit of a problem. Using hand gestures, Boris motioned Tom into the factory. He rightly assumed that the new man would want to see what Western had spent all of their money on.

When Tom walked through the door into the manufacturing area, it rapidly became apparent why the Bulgarians were so far ahead of the field in roller skate production. Practically all of the space within the factory was taken up by the biggest machine that Tom had ever set his eyes on.

At one end, people were shovelling in scrap metal, rubber and plastic, and at the other end, far in the distance, roller skates were being spat out onto a pile on the factory floor. Everything had been automated to the nth degree.

Tom had been briefed by the board of Western to report on how many skates a day the factory could produce and how much they cost to make. He tried to ask Boris what the numbers were, but Boris just looked at him in much the same way that a dog looks at you when you are trying to explain the principles of aerodynamics to it.

Tom tried asking in a louder voice and then tried speaking more slowly, but it made no difference.

Eventually by using a calendar, making a display of counting on his fingers, showing the notes in his wallet and pointing at the pile of skates on the floor it seemed that Boris understood him.

Boris found a piece of paper and drew a clock with a number 24 beside it. Underneath, he drew a roller skate with the number 3,000 beside it and under that he drew a dollar sign and another number. Tom gratefully took all of this information and phoned it through to Western.

When the accountants at the other end of the phone line had done their sums, they were quite pleased. Their new Bulgarian factory could produce around 85,000 roller skates a month at a reasonable cost and they instructed Tom to send the first order to them of 100,000 skates in five weeks time.

For the next few weeks Tom busied himself with settling in to his new home. Other than arranging for the transportation of 100,000 roller skates and phoning Western once a day to lie to them about how hard he was working, he didn't have much else to do. Under Boris's supervision the machine practically ran itself and Tom would pop in every afternoon to see that things were OK. This consisted of giving Boris a thumbs up and as Boris replied with the same gesture, everything seemed to be running smoothly.

It was only when they were getting ready to send the first delivery to Western that it became apparent that there was a problem. The pile of roller skates at the far end of the factory looked much larger than Tom had expected. He went to find Boris. When he found him, he made a show of counting on his fingers and pointing at the heap of roller skates. He then wrote the number 100,000 on a piece of paper.

Boris nodded and gave him thumbs up.

This wasn't right. Tom had been in the industry long enough to know what a pile of 100,000 roller skates looked like and the small mountain in front of him contained many more than that. He picked a skate from the pile and wrote 100,000 on the bottom of it and showed it to Boris. He in turn took another skate from the pile, put both of them in a box, and wrote 100,000 on the lid. When Tom had first asked him how many skates the factory produced per day Boris had written the number of pairs. They were always sold in pairs and it was logical to him that this was the number he had been asked for.

There were actually 200,000 roller skates in front of them and not the 100,000 that Tom had expected. This presented Tom with a problem. He could hardly confess to Western that his Bulgarian was so non-existent that he did not know that the factory was producing twice as many skates as he had been reporting. Still every cloud has a silver lining. They could simply switch the machine off for a month and send 100,000 this month and 100,000 next month. He pointed at the machine and made a cut throat signal.

Boris was horrified. He explained passionately and at great length to Tom that to switch off the machine would be the height of folly. All of the liquid metal and rubber would solidify and it would take months to strip it down, repair it and re set it up again.

Tom had no idea what he was talking about and when he went to pull the plug out of the wall, Boris stood in front of it so that he couldn't get to it and refused to budge. After a five minute standoff, Tom realised that he would have to find a better way to communicate with Boris.

He decided to let the machine keep running for the time being and he would figure out what to do later.

For now his priority was to make sure that Western just got half of the skates that were laying before him. He drew 2 skates on a piece of paper and then tore it in half. He raised one half of the torn paper pointed at it and said "Western." He then screwed up the other half and tossed it away.

Boris seemed to understand, and so Tom went off to try to think of a way out of the production / communication problem.

Boris Hoota could not understand why Tom wanted him to throw away half of the skates, but then he had not really understood him from day one. Still, it was no longer his business and in a few more weeks, he would be retiring and could leave Tom to it. So he sent 100,000 right-footed roller skates to Western and dumped 100,000 left-footed skates in his back yard.

He remarked to Olga that night that there must be a lot of one legged skaters where Tom came from.

The arrival of 100,000 useless unsalable roller skates tipped The Western Skate Co. over the edge.

They halted production and filed for bankruptcy on the same day they sacked Tom Smith. The once mighty Company was now only the owner of a Bulgarian skate factory that contained a rapidly cooling machine that could not be put back into operation for months and a pile of useless right-footed roller skates.

Boris Hoota read in his copy of Rollerski (Rollerski's Katatarba Ha, Skatedun nipa Ha) that his old factory was up for sale at a bargain price and that there were 100,000 worthless right-footed roller skates up for grabs as well. He gazed at the 100,000 left footed skates lying in his backyard, and thought that he might make the receivers an offer.

***

The Man Who Saved The World

© Anne Warwick 2011

*I*t seems that wherever you go nowadays you're tripping over a comic book hero. Only the other day I went down to the supermarket to buy a new washing-up bowl and had to fight my way through spidermen and wonder-women, all busy loading their baskets with mop buckets and fondue sets in order to secure my purchase. Even the girl on the check-out had a badge which read: Super-market cashier!

That's not to say that I am against these people. Where would we be if whenever we couldn't find our car keys we were unable to call up Super lost car key man, or worse, still pass adolescence without having Catwoman or Superman as a fantasy figure. It's just that there are so many of them and, contrary to popular perception, not one of them has actually managed to save the world. In fact the only person who has saved mankind from destruction was not a superhero at all. He was a rather grubby, dishonest clerk who worked in an insurance office. His name was Barry Duff and until now his story has never been told.

It all happened during the Cuban missile crisis of 1962.

Most of the history books will have you believe that what happened was that the Soviet Union transported some very large fireworks to the island of Cuba and pointed them at the United States. The Americans, who were not used to people pointing weapons at them, (collectively at least), became somewhat upset about this and President Kennedy had a row with President Khrushchev. Kennedy won the argument and the Soviets took all of their missiles back to Russia and pointed them at Germany instead. This of course is absolute rubbish.

What really happened was that since the end of the Second World War and the advent of the atomic bomb, both America and the Soviet Union had been building up considerable stocks of nuclear weapons and had not had the chance to use them and there is no point giving generals new weapons to play with and then not allowing them to light the blue touch paper. It's a bit like giving an eight-year-old child the toy of their dreams for Christmas, but not letting them take it out of the box.

In 1962 there were no major wars in progress and with no wars to fight, generals start getting irritable. At best, this means that they spend a lot of time moaning about their pension schemes and at worst, it means a military coup; neither option being particularly desirable.

Therefore the two great super-powers decided that a small limited nuclear war between themselves would be a good way to allow the generals to let off steam.

The beauty of a limited nuclear war was that it could all be over and done with, in a day. Not only that, but all of the hardware had already been bought and paid for, so it could be done on the cheap. By tea-time all of the surviving combatants would get lots of medals and America could then get on with building ridiculously large cars and Russia could get on with bringing in the turnip harvest.

But where to stage it?

As there was an element of danger involved and the best defence against being flash fried by a nuclear weapon is to be a long way away from it when it explodes, it needed to be a long way away from both Washington and Moscow. Western Europe was quickly ruled out as they were still paying back the money that they had borrowed from America for the last major conflict and the Americans were wary of destroying their future instalments. Brazil and West Africa were on the cards for a while, but the disruption to the coffee and chocolate markets ruled them out as well. They toyed with the idea of lobbing boxes of instant sunshine at each other over the Bering Strait, but the proximity of Canada scrubbed that one. Eventually a breakthrough came when Fidel Castro, the communist dictator of Cuba, said that they could use his place. This would be ideal. The Russians could fire their missiles at Florida (long way from Washington) and blow apart a large area of mosquito infested swampland and the Americans could wipe out Cuba (long way from Moscow). It also had the added bonus of destroying a five and a half-foot high irritating mouse that spent its time annoying visitors to a theme park in Orlando.

Now you may ask why Fidel Castro would have been so stupid as to allow his homeland to be obliterated by someone whom he was not at war with. Admittedly, he and Khrushchev were very pally, but friendship does not usually extend to the point that one allows one's best pal to instigate the destruction of all of your possessions. Castro, however, was not worried. Indeed, he was quite looking forward to seeing his homeland sink into the waters of the Caribbean because he was fully insured and when the radio-active dust had settled, he could buy a bigger and better island with the insurance money.

All really big things — Ships, jumbo jets, skyscrapers, nation states, etc — are insured with Lloyd's of London and as Castro had already received a red letter from Lloyd's telling him that his insurance was overdue, he sent the Cuban ambassador in London around to pay the bill.

The ambassador duly walked down to Lloyd's offices where he handed over a large bag of cash to settle the account.

All would have been well, except that the person he handed the money over to was the hero of our story who happened to be manning the front desk at the time.

Barry Duff didn't wear his underpants over his trousers, he didn't have x-ray vision, and was unable to fly without the use of an aeroplane, but what he did have was an unpaid gas bill amounting to three pounds, ten shillings and sixpence that was owed to the London Gas Board and in emulation of the fiscal policy of the Cuban leader, he hadn't paid it.

Barry was concerned that if his gas was cut off, he wouldn't be able to heat any water in his flat and despite looking under the mattress, down the back of the sofa and in all of his jacket pockets, he had been unable to come up with the necessary coinage and so to ease matters, instead of handing Castro's money in to the cashier's office, he paid the gas bill with some of it, hid the rest and planned to pay it in, together with the shortfall, when he received his pay-check at the end of the month.

During the next fortnight, America and Russia got ready to launch their missiles and were only 48 hours away from controlled Armageddon when Fidel Castro received a letter from Lloyd's informing him that his insurance was now out of date and therefore invalid. As a result of this letter Castro who, the day before, had been egging Khrushchev on to destroy the imperialist dogs to the north, now informed his political soul-mate that the war was off and that he would have to take all of his missiles back. He also mentioned in passing that as there were a lot more Cubans in Cuba than Russians, if he didn't take them back then Castro would take them himself.

Dictators can be very fickle at times.

Khrushchev, seething with rage, had little choice but to comply.

The Americans were a bit disappointed as well and tried to put a gloss on it by giving out the well known story of Kennedy winning the argument with Khrushchev.

In many ways it was as well that the mutually agreed nuclear strike did not take place, as in their eagerness to get started, both great powers had overlooked the interest that the smaller nations were taking in the unfolding situation. The U.S.A. and the U.S.S.R. were not the only people who had bored generals and nuclear weapons and once the shooting had started, both Britain and France were hoping to fire the odd one off when everyone was looking the other way. If this had happened, the conflict would have escalated and much of civilisation would have been wiped out.

In the years that followed, inter-continental ballistic missiles were developed, which meant that all of the major players could hit each other from launch sites within their own borders; thus ensuring that no individual was likely to start a nuclear war as they would be unlikely to be around when the victory parades were taking place at the end of it.

The nuclear powers were therefore forced to enter conventional foreign wars as ways of keeping their generals occupied.

The World which had held its breath during the course of the Cuban missile crisis and had started to go a bit red in the face could now exhale.

Unfortunately, we still have the mouse.

***

JANVIA'S WINDMILL

The country of Janvia is one of those places that have never been colonized by a foreign power. This is mainly because it's such a ghastly, inhospitable dump that nobody ever wanted. That's not to say that it's an ugly place. It has an abundance of rivers, lakes and gently rolling hills. If you saw a post-card of Janvia, you might truthfully say that it looked quite pretty. The problem is that by a freak of geology, Janvia is subject to a constant east-west wind that never subsides below gale force. This makes life fairly restrictive, in that the eating of soup or ice cream in the open air is nigh on impossible.

If you were to take out the large encyclopaedia that your aunt gave you for your birthday a few years ago and looked up the description of Janvia, it would read something like this:

JANVIA, unaligned independent democracy.

Population: 1.6 million.

Resources: Arable farming.

Exports: Potatoes, turnips, beetroot, kites.

If you looked in the super giant encyclopaedia in the library, you could also learn that Janvia had the lowest number of tumble driers per head of population and the greatest expenditure, per head of population, on roof tiles.

The Janvians themselves are quite fond of their homeland; much in the same way that a shepherd may be fond of an old faithful dog that's become lame — just before he shoots it.

They write songs and poems about the rivers and hills and the trees that grow at 45 degrees and about how great it will be when the wind dies down a bit.

Janvia is a relatively young nation. The land had always been there of course, but the border lines had not been drawn onto maps until the previous century.

A flag had been knitted by the wife of the first president. It is a blue rectangle with a picture of a Bogo bird in the centre; an animal found nowhere else in the world. An interesting thing to note about the Bogo bird is that it has very powerful legs. The reason for this is that, although it can fly great distances at high speed from east to west, the wind is so strong that it normally has to walk back home.

When it was realised that the country's 100th birthday was approaching, the politicians wanted to do something to mark the occasion. They wanted to do something big, something impressive, something that would show the world that Janvia was at the cutting edge, something to bring the tourists in. It had to be a monumental structure of some sort.

Obviously, it could not be a skyscraper or a bridge; it had to be something else.

A competition was held in the newspapers; to find a suitably impressive, monumental, tourist-inducing thing to build. The winning entry was a suggestion to build the world's biggest windmill. This would have two distinct benefits. Firstly, it would provide free electricity to the people of Janvia and secondly, it would give tourists something to look at. They would be able to say to each other on their return home, "OK honey, I know that we may have spent our vacation in a ghastly, unpleasant, inhospitable, draughty dump, but hey! Wasn't that some windmill!"

Due to its lack of oil wells, gold mines, off shore banking etc., Janvia didn't have the capital available to build the windmill from its own resources and had to go to the bank for a loan. The money would be paid back by keeping the electricity bills at the same level as before, and, the accountants figured that after 23 years, the people of Janvia would be in receipt of free electricity. Everybody agreed that this would be a splendid thing.

Once the money was in place, work on building the world's biggest windmill began.

Such a big building needed to be of exceptional strength to withstand the constant winds and so the windmill was built using ton after ton of reinforced concrete, which arrived by the truck load in a fetching shade of bunker grey.

When finished, the building had walls 40-ft thick. It was impressively strong. It was also exceptionally high and could be seen for a distance of more than 20 miles. The Janvians had created something of which they could be justifiably proud.

At the unveiling ceremony, the chocks were knocked away from the massive sails and the windmill churned into life; the sails rotating faster and faster until they were just a blur. Electricity flowed and the people partied long into the night in celebration.

After a while, everyone got used to the windmill being always in the background. It became part of the scenery. It also gave a boost to the tourist industry; the number of visitors rising from a lamentable 8 per year to an impressive 27. The old brochure that the tourist board had issued before used to say : COME TO BEAUTIFUL WIND SWEPT JANVIA . But now it said: COME TO BEAUTIFUL WIND SWEPT JANVIA AND GAZE IN WONDER AT OUR WINDMILL.

After a while, Mrs. Stuckheimer, who ran the guest house opposite, was able to trade in her old car for a slightly newer one.

The problems began 22 years and 6 months after the windmill had first started to operate. After so much time, the bearings had worn and the windmill had started to issue a low screeching noise. In the weeks that followed, the noise became louder and louder, until people were unable to sleep for it. What was worse, the few tourists that visited normally left within the first hour. It was decided that the windmill would have to be closed down while repairs were made.

Unfortunately, when the windmill had been built, although much thought had gone into the structure of the building, very little thought had gone into the machinery that had been installed inside. It was discovered that the windmill not only lacked an integrated braking system, but it lacked a breaking system of any kind at all.

The nation's finest engineers stood around and scratched their heads, trying to think of a way to stop the sails turning while all the time the screeching from the thing was getting worse and worse. They tried putting sticks in between the sails, but they were snatched from their hands and tossed away by the force of the machine. They then tried bigger sticks, then gate posts and finally telegraph poles, but nothing worked. The only thing they could suggest was to demolish the whole thing with explosives. This would mean the end of the free electricity that people were expecting in a few months time, but at least the noise would stop and the tourists would stay. After much soul-searching, the government reluctantly agreed to this solution. At least with the blowing up of such a large building, they could expect tourists from all over the world to come and see it happen.

There was only one pyrotechnical engineer in Janvia. His name was Joe Gladys. He normally drove a tractor and just dabbled in explosives in his spare time. Firework displays are not very popular in a place where, after you have sent a rocket into the sky, it explodes 10 miles downwind. But as there was only the one man, he got the job to demolish the windmill. Explosives, wire and igniters were sourced and books were consulted on the amount of explosive material to use. After a week, the windmill was primed for demolition. There would be a further one week delay while television cameras were set up, politicians rehearsed their speeches and the final few tourists arrived to witness the spectacle. During this time, the politicians had worried that, if the windmill was not destroyed at the first attempt, they would be made to look foolish and had ordered that an extra 10% of plastic explosive be added. Joe Gladys also wanted his biggest job to date to be a success and added another 10% himself just to be on the safe side.

On the appointed day, a small crowd of onlookers,

politicians and TV crews assembled outside of Mrs. Stuckheimer's guest house to witness the big moment. Thus it was that at 2 P.M. on a glorious Saturday afternoon, marred only by a howling gale and a screeching windmill, the igniter button was pressed.

Had Joe not neglected to put a decimal point in his calculations on the amount of explosive to use and packed just 2 tons of explosive into the building, rather than the 24 tons that actually got used, the resulting explosion would not have been as spectacular as that witnessed on that fateful Saturday. The blast that took place not only demolished the windmill, it also broke every window for a radius of five miles and could be heard 120 Miles away. Mrs. Stuckheimer was so upset that she retired to the toilet at the end of her garden and when she pulled the chain, the ceiling, which had been weakened by the blast, fell in on top of her.

Janvia is still a beautiful place; although there's not much to look at apart from a demolished windmill. Also, the lights don't work as there's no electricity and ordering a drink or a meal is difficult as every-one is deaf.

But if you are looking for somewhere to fly your kite, then Janvia's the place for you.

***

ROMEO SONNYMYRA

It was appropriate that Nancy Sonnymyra should die in public, although the exact time of her death was difficult to ascertain. This was because she died during a formal dinner hosted by the local industrial society and no-one noticed that she had stopped breathing until she slowly slumped forward in her seat, culminating in her face sinking into a plate of sherry trifle.

It was remarked afterwards that because of her known meanness, most people were surprised that she hadn't waited until the coffee and mints had been served before expiring.

Until that moment, Nancy had been the major shareholder of Cleveland Work-wear, a highly profitable distributor of hard-wearing, reasonably priced clothing.

As far as most people were aware, Nancy had no heirs and she had been such an unpleasant domineering old rat-bag that no-one had had the courage to enquire if she had any offspring. Nancy herself never mentioned any children and everybody assumed that she had been as cold in her romantic dealings with men as she had been on matters of business. It was therefore with some interest that the board of Cleveland waited for the reading of Nancy's will in order to discover who their new owner would be.

Much to everyone's surprise, it turned out that Nancy had actually given birth to a child. It had happened fifty years earlier during a grand tour of Europe. The birth had taken place in Turin and the child had been named Romeo. It appeared that when Nancy returned from Italy, she had left the baby there in the care of a paid nanny and over the years, she had sent considerable sums of money to Italy to provide for the care of her child and had also set up a generous trust fund for him.

She had kept his existence a secret for half a century. Nancy's will left all of her shareholding to her son.

A company lawyer was despatched to Italy to locate Nancy's son and break the sad news of his mother's death and the somewhat more cheerful news that he was now a multi-millionaire.

After some discussion, the company board issued statement to the press, stating that the company would continue to be a family business and that the major shareholding had passed to Nancy's son, Romeo.

The managing director commented ruefully that he hoped that the son would be a bit more user-friendly than the mother had been.

The name Sonnymyra is not a common one. Even less so is the name Romeo Sonnymyra, but there was one man in Cleveland who had it. He worked as a junior quality control inspector at the Chocco Crunch breakfast cereal factory. American Romeo spent his days watching box after box of breakfast cereal trundle past him. Every so often he would take a box from the line, check the printing, open the top of the box and check the bag inside. If everything was as it should be, he would then re-seal it and send another 15 tons of the stuff through. The job was so mind-numbingly boring that he would occasionally slip a note into the box before re-sealing it. The notes varied from "Enjoy your breakfast." to "Get me out of here." The only distraction he had while working was the radio that blared away without interruption during the 8 hour shift and was permanently tuned to KTFM. Romeo knew the names of every daytime DJ, every news reporter and every word of every advertising jingle.

On the day of the Cleveland Work-wear press release, Romeo made his way home from the breakfast cereal factory as usual. When he reached his apartment he saw that there was a man standing outside, apparently waiting for him.

"Romeo Sonnymyra?" The man said. Romeo wondered if he owed the man some money.

"Yes," he said cautiously.

"Today's a good day for you," the man said, thrusting a tape recorder under Romeo's nose.

Romeo relaxed. Now it all made sense. The phrase "It's a good day for you" was used by the radio station. They sent people out onto the street with recorders and if you replied, "Yes I listen to KTFM," they gave you 50 bucks.

"Yes I listen to KTFM." he said.

The man looked a little taken aback, but quickly recovered. "How will the money change your life?" he asked. Romeo considered the question.

"Not that much," he said "I might take in a baseball game."

The man produced a camera and asked Romeo if he would pose for a picture.

"Sure," said Romeo putting on his best grin.

With his photo and his quote safely recorded, the newspaper reporter — for that's what he was — thanked Romeo for his time and hurried off down the road.

It took Romeo a few moments before he realised that he had not been paid.

"Hey! Where's my fifty bucks!" He yelled at the retreating figure.

The following day, Romeo's photograph, together with a short article, appeared in the business section of the newspaper. The headline read: "CLEVELAND HEIR JUST A REGULAR GUY."

Romeo didn't see it. He, and just about everyone else at the breakfast cereal factory, never read the business section.

The working day passed in the same mind-numbing way as normal, the only difference being that Romeo shouted at the radio a lot.

There were other people, however, who had seen the article and a few days later, Romeo's photograph, together with a re-write of the original report, found its way into the general news section of the newspapers.

One of the other workers at the factory showed it to him.

Romeo was astounded. He had got his photo in the newspaper only once before and that was only due to a culmination of errors that ended with his house being accidentally demolished instead of the one next door. The newspaper had obviously made a mistake and Romeo laughed along with everyone else at the absurdity of the report. Although when he got home that night, he found the owner of the local Ford dealership waiting for him with yet another photographer and a new car that the man was prepared to loan him for a year; all for the price of having his photo taken. Romeo thought it prudent to keep quiet. It might be a couple of weeks before the car dealer realised his mistake and asked for it back, and it wouldn't hurt to drive a new car for a while.

On the same day that Romeo was gratefully accepting the keys to a new Ford, Cleveland's lawyer was briefing the company management on his meeting with their new owner.

Italian Romeo had received the news of his mother's death quite calmly, although as he had only come into contact with her very rarely, that was perhaps not surprising.

He had spent his entire life eating the finest food and drinking the finest wine. He spent each summer on the beaches of southern France and passed the winters in the ski resorts of the Italian Alps.

His mother had provided well for him, to the extent that he had never had the need to worry about where the next Lamborghini was coming from. Unfortunately, he had inherited his mother's looks as well as her money, which at least proves that there is some justice in the world. He was pleased to learn of the shares that he had inherited and after he had given the matter some thought, he had decided that he would slowly sell them over the next twenty years. He had no knowledge of clothing retail or of any other type of business for that matter and was not particularly keen to learn. He had never worked a day in his life nor had he before he had the burden of running a business and he had no intention of starting now. Provided that the management of Cleveland continued to keep the company on an even keel, he was quite happy to let them get on with it.

This was good news for the management of the company as they could continue trading as before without damaging interference from outside.

Things seemed to have resolved themselves very well.

The board breathed a communal sigh of relief and looked at the remainder of the agenda for the meeting. The final item was: 'What do we do about the breakfast cereal inspector that the newspapers were claiming as the new company boss?'

They had read all of the newspaper reports, but had not commented on them until they knew where they stood in relation to Italian Romeo.

Now that they had full effective control of the company, they debated what to do.

The simplest thing would be just to issue a statement denouncing American Romeo as an imposter, but then again, they might be able to use the feel-good stories in the newspapers to their advantage.

American Romeo was a typical average guy and looked the part, whereas Italian Romeo was a spoilt greasy over-weight foreigner with a high pitched voice who had never worn any Cleveland Work-ware products and was unlikely to do so. If they could get American Romeo, the regular blue collar guy from next door to work for them as a spokesman, it would give the company a good image and help sales. The public already thought that he was the owner and providing that the company did nothing to disillusion them, who would be the wiser. If asked, they could just say that the company was owned by Romeo Sonnymyra.

They were not going to lie. They would just be a bit economical with the truth.

Thus it was, that American Romeo was contacted by Cleveland Work-wear and offered a job as company spokesman with triple his previous salary from the breakfast cereal factory and the gift of a rent free apartment on the top floor of Cleveland's office block.

Unsurprisingly, Romeo did not have to think about it for long before he accepted the offer. He was given a personal assistant by the company and in a reversal of the normal roles, his personal assistant told him what to do rather than the other way round. He was simply there to wear the products, smile at the cameras and say what he had been told to say.

He picked it up quickly, and within a matter of months, his face was known across the country.

People referred to him as Mr. Cleveland. His unassuming stance and his simple straight forward way of speaking made him popular with the people that bought working clothes; sales and profits grew as a result.

After six months, it was decided to send Romeo and his personal assistant on a morale-boosting visit to the company's main production site in India. The usual posse of TV and newspaper reporters were invited to report on the event.

Romeo found himself standing in a huge unventilated factory just outside of Calcutta. In front of him sat row upon row of grim faced women hunched over sewing machines. Porters pushed wheeled tubs of finished and partly finished clothing, hither and thither. As he stood watching the repetitive actions of the women, Romeo's eyes stung as sweat dripped into them and his ears rang with the noise of a thousand buzzing sewing machines. It reminded him of his life in the breakfast cereal factory, except that it was ten times more unpleasant. Despite the intense heat, he felt a cold anger rising in him.

A week later, the board of Cleveland had assembled for an emergency meeting. Before each one of them was a copy of that morning's business press. The main headline screamed out at them, "MR. CLEVELAND PLEDGES US STANDARDS IN OVERSEAS FACTORIES."

The managing director called the meeting to order. The first item on the agenda before him was:

'What do we do about Sonnymyra?'

***

THE EASTER BUNNY

© Anne Warwick 2011

*E*veryone loved the Easter Bunny. "What a fine little chap," they would say as he busied himself hiding eggs in gardens and back yards across the land.

He was so well thought of that he had songs and poems written about him. He had also appeared on high value postage stamps in Finland, was a close confidant of King Juan Carlos of Spain and had been voted best loved personality every year for fifteen years running by the Chocolate Manufacturers Guild.

Yes, everyone loved the Easter Bunny — except the chickens.

They hated him.

As far as the chickens were concerned, eggs were their business and the Easter Bunny — cute and fluffy as he may be — had no right to muscle in on their territory. If anyone was going to hide eggs it should be them. Rabbits and eggs indeed! The idea was absurd.

They started a campaign to regain their rights.

To be fair to the chickens, they did have a strong case and it was logical that egg-laying poultry had more claim on egg-related issues than non-egg-laying rodents.

They hen-pecked the "powers that be" until they were given the sole rights to worldwide egg secretion. As a result, although the Easter Bunny had managed to hang on to the film and TV rights, he nevertheless found himself out of a job.

Now the Easter Bunny had been hiding eggs for all of his life, as had his father and grandfather before him. He knew nothing else.

They sent him on a course to retrain as a missing sock retriever, but his heart was not in it. While the lecturer was droning on about the importance of sock shade, Bunny would be staring out of the window day-dreaming of hiding eggs behind trees.

Some might say that it was an obsession on his part, but he had been bred to it and the thought of life without eggs was unbearable to him. He began to sneak into supermarkets and take the eggs from the shelf and hide them behind the freezer that contained the fish fingers.

During the evening he would creep undetected into restaurants and move the eggs from the fridge and put them into the pockets of the jackets that were hanging on the coat rack. He knew that he was doing wrong, but he couldn't help it. People began to get annoyed with him. Every time you left a restaurant and put your hand in your pocket for your car keys, it would come out covered in runny egg.

They demanded that something be done and so the Police came and arrested the Easter Bunny.

He was brought before the magistrate and found guilty of unlawful egg rearrangement and sent to prison. The magistrate also told him that if he was naughty again, it would be rabbit stew time. For a rabbit, this was dire news indeed.

The thing about Easter is that it arrives all of a sudden without you expecting it; a bit like the 6th Panzer Grenadier Division. It certainly caught the chickens off guard. They had not thought out the logistics of hiding eggs and they had not realized that their lack of paws prevented them from transporting them.

Once the eggs had been laid, the chickens did what chickens do and sat on them.

Unlike other years when you really had to search hard to find hidden eggs in your garden, now all you needed to do was locate a chicken and lift it up and underneath you would find the eggs.

As chickens, by dint of their size, were easier to spot than eggs, things became too easy and all of the fun went out of it. People became disheartened. What had once been a mildly interesting afternoon now became a dull ten minutes.

The chickens were not very happy either. Every five minutes someone would be lifting them up and peering underneath them. I mean, how would you like it? There you are sitting nice and quiet, when all of a sudden someone grabs you by the throat, lifts you off the floor and either takes away what you were sitting on or looks up your bottom!

Chickens are rarely happy at the best of times and now they demanded that the Easter Bunny be released from prison. As far as they were concerned he could have his old job back with pleasure.

They clucked and moaned until their demands were met.

Now rabbits aren't just good at hiding eggs. They are good at other things as well. (No not that!) — and when the prison guards opened the cell door, they found that the cell was empty save for a rabbit hole in the middle of the floor.

The temptation to hide eggs had been too great for the Easter Bunny and he had started to tunnel his way to freedom.

They shouted down the rabbit hole that if he came back, they would release him and give him his old job back. The Easter Bunny heard them, but he also remembered the magistrate's words.

Breaking out of prison was a serious crime and he didn't want to be served up as someone's dinner.

He kept burrowing away until he emerged not very far away from your back garden.

This Easter he'll be back hiding eggs in gardens and back yards, but you will never see him. He is careful now and no longer trusts what people say and he is afraid of the stew pot.

***

ACCOUNTANCY DONKEYS

You don't see many donkeys around nowadays. It's not that surprising of course, a donkey can carry less than a mule, it runs slower than a horse and provides neither milk, nor meat.

At one time, practically every other household had a donkey in the garden, but no longer. This is entirely due to the invention of the pocket calculator of course.

You see, donkeys may not be much use as providers of hamburger meat, but they are fantastically good at mathematics and before pocket calculators came along, people would keep a donkey in order to help them plan the family finances. If you had a really difficult sum to do — how many spoons you would have left after a divorce settlement perhaps — then the donkey would be able to tell you the number exactly. Bah! You might say the number of spoons left would be easy to calculate; it would be half the number you started with. If you had twenty spoons before the ex-love of your life sheered off in a different direction from you, then you would end up with ten. However, if you asked the donkey what the number would be, he would tell you either the number nine or the number eleven and he would always be right. This is because not only are donkeys very good at maths, they are also brilliant at reading human nature. The donkey would know, which one of the humans would pinch an extra spoon from their partner out of spite or greed thus altering the obvious number. All very useful if you are going to have a dinner party to celebrate your divorce and have invited nine other people along to it.

Donkeys are so good at this sort of thing that all businesses connected with finance used to employ them. In the 1960's, if you asked your bank manager for a loan, he would normally pop out the back to discuss it with the bank's donkey before returning to say that you couldn't have any money.

It all changed following NASA's successful Apollo moon missions. NASA took the decision very early on not to involve donkeys in the planning or execution of all of their missions. They figured that they had enough computing power to work out how to get an oversized metal trash-can from earth to wherever it was going and back again without having to check with a donkey every five minutes. They were perfectly right in this assumption. The space missions were planned as an engineering problem and human instinct was kept to an absolute minimum. Although astronauts were used, they were all highly disciplined former air force pilots extensively trained to do exactly what they were told to do. If you had put a plumber on board of Apollo 11, he would had spent the first ten minutes pressing all the buttons and messing about with the cassette player and the thing would never have got off the ground.

The space programme generated a huge amount of interest, as well as a number of useful spin-offs including the non-stick frying pan and affordable pocket calculators. The banks and finance houses thought that if NASA could put a man on the moon without recourse to donkeys, then working out Mr. Jones' mortgage payments using the now widely available calculators could be done in the same manner.

As the donkeys retired from their individual service in the financial sector they were replaced by people using computers and calculators, although it is believed that the IRS still keep a few in the back yard just in case they have some really difficult sums to do.

Donkeys were seen as old fashioned and anachronistic. If you wanted to be at the cutting edge of the new technological age, you got rid of your donkey and went down to the local store and bought a pocket calculator. As a result donkeys began to disappear both from gardens and also from the collective psyche. The donkeys that remained were banished to the countryside and relegated to calculating the growth rate of the grass that they stood on.

Now individual donkeys are quite placid creatures; they don't ask for much out of life. Give them an amusing straw hat and a handful of carrots and they're reasonably happy. But collectively they are a different proposition entirely.

As donkeys fell more and more out of favour, even the meagre fare of straw hats and carrots began to dry up and large numbers of donkeys found themselves in donkey sanctuaries. Within these close confines, the seeds of revolutionary fervour were sown by a disgruntled old donkey by the name of Sally, who at one time had been the steadying force behind the Chief of the Federal Reserve.

With her oratory skills, Sally incited the other donkeys into taking punitive retaliation against the people who had treated them so shabbily. Over the next few years, heavily disguised donkeys infiltrated their way into the major finance houses across the world. This was fairly straightforward as most of the human workers were so engrossed in their work that they rarely glanced up from the computer screen and those that did, barely registered the fact that they might be sitting next to a donkey. For as anyone who has worked in international finance will know, most bankers on Wall Street have long hairy faces and big ears — including some of the men.

The donkey's grasp of human nature was put to stunning effect. Not only were they able to add numbers together, and manage the even more difficult task of taking numbers away, but by writing large numbers down on reports and adding dollar signs they were able to exploit the twin weaknesses of all bankers; those of laziness and greed.

They proposed that if the banks lent money which they did not have, to people who could not pay it back, guaranteed by property that was worth less than the money lent on it, the banks would somehow make money out of it all. It has to be said that they did not put the case quite like that and hid the actual meaning within the pages of voluminous proposal documents, but as the people they were pitching it to only read the figures on the front and back pages, it didn't matter. The banks embarked on a lending frenzy.

Within a year, it had all gone horribly wrong for the banks. The people they had lent money to had squandered some of it on food and utility bills and had been unable to re-pay the banks, who now became the possessors of properties that were worth less than the amount that they had been bought for and as it had been notional money rather than the real folding stuff that had bought said properties, they were forced to sell at a loss thus bankrupting themselves. It was doubly ironic because there was nobody to buy the houses back from them as no-one could now get a loan from the bank to buy things with.

Some of the donkeys were paid off by the banks and forced to leave, but they didn't care. They had made their point and knew that the humans were too vain to admit that they were wrong and too proud to ask the donkeys to help them resolve the problem. They returned to the donkey sanctuaries with enough money to keep them in straw hats and carrots for years. The remainder stayed at the banks and finance houses entertaining themselves by writing more and more absurd proposals to recover the money they themselves had caused the humans to lose.

So if you have found yourself the owner of a worthless house, or homeless, or unemployed or broke because of the recession, at least you have the comfort of knowing it is due to the greed of the bankers and the donkeys they employ.

***

Internet Shed

© Anne Warwick 2011

It is a little known fact that the internet was invented in 1973 for the sole reason that Mrs. Briggs was sick of walking to the shed at the bottom of the garden to tell her husband that his tea was ready.

Of course, it is written in the Magna Carta that it is every Englishman's birthright to have a shed and Norman Briggs was particularly fond of his. When not arranging screws in boxes or taking toasters apart, he would spend most of his time there watching old black and white movies on a small portable television.

His wife did not mind that he spent so much time in the shed, but resented having to take her curlers out before she walked down the garden in case Mrs. Fredrice next door saw her.

She confronted her husband about this one night and the next day, Norman set about creating a communication system that would eventually evolve into the World Wide Web.

Within 2 days, he had achieved his task by nailing together an electric typewriter, a fax machine and a TV screen. Fortunately, all his nails and screws were in the right boxes, otherwise it would have taken him much longer.

From her work station next to the washing machine

in the kitchen, Mrs. Briggs could now pass information to her husband in the shed without having to remove her curlers.

The very first e-mail sent that would change the way that the world communicated forever was:

"Your dinner is ready and if you are not here in 5 minutes, I'm going to give it to the dog."

When the message flashed up on Norman's TV screen half way through his viewing of The 39 Steps, he immediately returned to the house and went to the dinner table.

Pavlov would have been proud.

News of the Briggs' new communication system soon spread to other people. Carol Drinkwater, the heavily made up blond who always seemed to have an extra button on her blouse undone, and lived 3 doors away, suggested that if she had a machine similar to that of Mrs. Briggs, the 2 women could gossip about Mrs. Fredrice without being overheard. As a result a new cable was passed to Norman's shed. He now had the task of passing on messages from one woman to the other. Thus it was that electronic messaging or e-mail was established. For the record the first message via the net was:

"Did you see the dress she was wearing yesterday? Honestly it made her look like an elephant."

As time went on, more and more people became connected to Norman's shed or the internet as it was more popularly known. After a while, there were so many cables running to the shed that it was difficult to squeeze through the door. Norman also found to his dismay that he was so busy receiving and sending messages that he hardly had time left to organise his jars of screws and bits of broken toaster.

"Honestly" He said to Mr. Ebay, who ran the second-hand shop near the gasworks, "It's getting too much. Sometimes, when I come back from the toilet, there can be more than 20 messages there waiting for me to send onto people."

Still, it was Norman's proud boast that he had only ever lost one message. He had copied it down on the back of his wife's shopping list and when she went to the shops with it and finished her shopping, she had given the list to someone who had forgotten to bring their own.

Norman decided that he had to try and sell the internet, so he placed a card in the local newsagent's window.

It read:

FOR SALE. WORLD-WIDE COMMUNICATION SYSTEM. ONE CAREFUL OWNER. MAINTAINED REGARDLESS OF COST. SERIOUS OFFERS INVITED.

He wasn't sure what sort of response he would get, so he paid an extra fifty pence to run the advert for 2 weeks.

After 10 days, the only response he had was from evil Mr. Chamberlain who owned the local meat canning factory and had invented spam. Norman did not really want to sell to him, but the task of running the internet was becoming a strain and he wanted to take his wife away for a short holiday.

Fortunately, he had a stroke of luck. Mr. Stratton from the cricket club had heard about Norman's problem and offered to look after the internet while Norman took his wife to Birmingham for the weekend to watch a wrestling match.

When they returned, Mr. Stratton offered to stay on and help out. With 2 people receiving and passing on e-mails, the system became twice as quick. Thus was born 'High Speed Internet'.

They are still there to this day, running the internet from the shed at the bottom of the garden. So each time you send an e-mail, don't forget that it's powered by Briggs and Stratton.

***

The Red Light District

© Anne Warwick 2011

$\mathcal{L}$indsey Beckingham-Hyde had always been fashionable.

She could not remember a time when she had not been. During her childhood in London's Mayfair and her education at the private school in Bloomsbury, she had always been clothed in high quality, fashionable garments.

Being close to all of the best stores helped, as did the very generous allowance from her wealthy parents. She mixed in the best of society and it was normal for her to regard the finest things in life as being things to which she had a right of birth. She could see no wrong in this. How could she! Every one of her friends was of the same select circle and she had no understanding of how others lived. If she were to think about it — which was rarely — she would blithely assume that the poor were poor through a lack of intelligence; rather than a lack of opportunity.

When Lindsey left her finishing school, her parents suggested that she find something to occupy her time with until the inevitable marriage to the offspring of one of their friends.

Lindsey regarded her greatest talent as the ability to select clothes and articles in fashionable colours and styles, and so it was not a great shock when she announced that she was going to be an interior designer. This would involve no manual labour or tiresome science, but merely the ability to express what was "in" at the moment and advise accordingly. She could charge her friends who were setting up home substantial fees for her services and when she ran out of them, there were plenty of rich influential people known to her parents who would employ her on various projects.

She was very successful in her chosen profession or art as she preferred to call it. To be fair to her, she did know at all times what the current expensive fad doing the rounds happened to be. When colours and fashions came in, she would advise her clients correctly and, over time, she became well known as a trend guru. This extended to having her own column ghost-written for her in some of the hyper-classy style magazines.

Thus, it was that when the executive board of the Pudford City Development Corporation were looking to spend a large amount of the taxpayers' money on revamping Pudford, they approached Lindsey and asked if she would act as an executive style adviser. It was thought that the inclusion of Miss Beckingham-Hyde would lend a certain class to the project. The very generous package that they offered included the proviso that Lindsey be seen to be involved at the highest level of decision making.

Lindsey herself was happy to oblige; the publicity would raise her iconic status even higher than it already was. She also agreed to move into Pudford's closest version of a luxury flat for the 12 months duration of the revitalisation project or at the very least, have some of her mail directed there.

Pudford City itself did not have a great deal going for it.

Miles away from anywhere of any importance, it was an ex-industrial sprawl of empty engineering factories and poor housing with no natural beauty to speak of. At one time, there had been a certain pride in being a Pudfordian, but no longer. When the industry went, the talented went with it and only the helpless, the old and the disenfranchised had remained.

At the first working meeting of the development corporation, Lindsey was asked her views on the best way to make Pudford City a world-class destination. She had been thinking about this for some time and it appeared to her that whatever was done, colours would play an important part. She had seen some absolutely exquisite lighting effects in some of the London art galleries and thought that the use of coloured lighting would be the first step in transforming Pudford from the dump it appeared to be into something more stylish. She expounded on this theory for some time and as a celebrity style guru, her thoughts carried immense importance. She explained that the vital thing was to use the right colours and as the colour currently in mode was red, it should be used extensively.

She suggested that some of the street lighting be changed from the current common white or yellow to red. This would give the public areas a warm friendly feel. The thoughts of Miss Lindsey Beckingham-Hyde were received very well by the assembled managers and administrators. None of whom, as well paid civil servants, had the misfortune to have to live in the place.

When the clerk of works was told that henceforth much of the city's public street-lights now needed to be changed to red, he thought that it was the most absurd idea he had ever heard of and said so.

He pointed out to the Implementation Director of the development corporation that as clerk of works, he had years of experience coupled with years of technical training and that there were very good reasons why the street lights were the colour that they were. In turn he was told that if he wanted to retain one of the few jobs in the area, he would do what he was told. He was paid to do things rather than interfere in strategy and he would do well to remember that fact. This argument was not lost on him and so he detailed the City workforce to change the bulbs in all of the street lights.

Much money was spent on publicizing Pudford's new lighting scheme and a lavish switching on ceremony was staged. When the new red street lights were switched on before an admiring press, they did indeed cast a warm glow across the city. Buildings and wastelands did indeed look less harsh when bathed in soft red lighting. It appeared that the money given to Miss Beckingham-Hyde had been well spent.

As any first year physics student will tell you, if you illuminate a room solely in red light and then switch on an additional red light, a table lamp with a red bulb say, you will not be able to distinguish the fact that said table lamp contains a red bulb; the colour simply will not be discernible. This is not a problem unless it is important that you identify that the light is red — such as on things like traffic lights and car brake lights.

During the first three weeks of operation, it was estimated

that Pudford's red lighting system caused 14 deaths, 345 serious injuries and cost the economy in excess of 30 million pounds.

As Lindsey sped back down the motorway in her Porsche to London, she thought ruefully to herself that it was a good thing that no-one of any importance in the capitol had ever heard of Pudford.

***

Howling Banjos

© Anne Warwick 2011

Dogs are pretty smart animals. They know that if they lay on the floor and put their legs in the air, sooner or later someone will come along and tickle their belly. They may even get a biscuit out of it as well.

Whenever Mrs. Johnson at number 36 lies on her back and puts her legs in the air, her husband just turns the TV on and starts to watch the sports channel.

Yes dogs have got it made. They sleep when they want, eat regular meals and do no work. OK, you may say "What about guard dogs? They work."

No they don't. What they do is lounge about and barks occasionally. It's not exactly putting in an 8 hour shift at the local uranium mine is it!

Over the last few thousand years, dogs have cleverly managed to train people to provide them with all of life's comforts without any of the stress.

They have taught people to feed them, house them, pet them and throw balls for them without having to give anything in return. Incredibly, people were quite happy with this arrangement until their banjos started to disappear.

You know when you put your banjo down, you can never find the damn thing again. This doesn't happen with guitars or trumpets. When you put your guitar down it always stays in the same place, but not your banjo. This is because your banjo has been stolen by a dog and you are unlikely ever to find your instrument again. As a result you are forced to go and buy another one.

Insurance firms know this of course.

As the idea of insurance is to give your money to the company rather than the other way round, you will see thousands of advertisements for insuring your house, car, life etc, but I bet that you have never seen an insurance company offering to insure your banjo. They know that it's not worth the risk and if you press them on it, they will look at the floor and mumble something about specialist markets and the waywardness of G strings.

Prior to 1928, dogs had not realized that they were musical, for the very good reason that they are not.

Dogs simply find it impossible to carry a tune. Even if you were to put it in a bucket and hang it around their necks for them, they would not be able to do it and so the sudden canine interest in 1928 for banjos is a bit of a mystery.

No-one knows why dogs were so attracted to banjos and why they show no interest in any other musical instrument.

Various theories have been put about, but none have come up with a satisfactory answer.

As dogs were unlikely to go to the trouble of learning to play a musical instrument, it came as no great surprise to find that the cacophony of sound from a banjo-playing dog could be best likened to that of the noise made by a traumatised cat being dragged through a combine harvester.

People started to lock their dogs out of their homes, and the dogs realized that if they wanted to keep their cushy number, they would have to restrict their banjo playing to times when there was no-one else around.

As they were no longer being seen playing banjos, in time, people forgot that their dogs had a secret obsession. Occasionally someone would come home early from work and catch their pet destroying 'Stairway to Heaven' on their missing banjo, but when they told others about it, they would not be believed.

Because people's banjos kept going missing, people could no longer practice with them and so spent more time playing the guitar instead. Had it not been for the fact that John Lennon had a dog named Trixie, popular music may well have not changed course in the way that it did.

As yesterday's fashion dictates what tomorrows will be, sales of guitars increased and banjo-based music declined. The sales of banjos were not greatly affected though, as each musician would have to buy a large number of banjos during their lifetime to replace the ones that had been stolen by their pets.

Once a dog had its paws on a banjo, it would not tune or maintain the instrument and would attempt to play the thing until the strings broke before burying it in the garden and before going to look for another one.

The dogs found themselves in an awkward position. If they came out and admitted their love of the banjo, it would be likely that the people who feed and cared for them would try and make them play the things properly. This would involve hours of work each day for no extra comfort or better food.

They had spent years conditioning people to do all the work for them and could see no reason why they should now have to start working for a living. So to this day, they have pretended to have no interest in musical instruments of any kind.

So the next time that you walk past an open window and the music from it sounds as though someone's dog is trying to play the banjo, don't worry, because that is probably exactly what's happening.

***

Britain's Last Pirate

When the tiny principality of Liechtenstein suddenly became the richest country on earth, due to a junior clerk at the world bank accidentally putting Germany's GDP into Liechtenstein's bank account, the grand duke of Liechtenstein did what anyone else who has suddenly come into more money than they could possibly ever spend and drew up a list of everyone who had hacked him off over the years.

It was not a very long list; the obvious reason being that it is unusual for people to be rude to minor royalty.

After he had thought about it for a week, the only people he could think of to hate was the English, as the year before, they had knocked Liechtenstein out of the world cup due to a dubious penalty decision.

The duke bought himself a very large expensive yacht. On the large expensive yacht, he installed a large expensive loudspeaker system and when all was ready, he sailed it up the English Channel and anchored just off the coast of Newhaven, where he settled down to shout rude things at the English people he could see walking their dogs along the cliff-tops.

This was somewhat upsetting to the dog walkers.

They would be quietly ambling along admiring the large expensive yacht off shore, when all of a sudden a heavily accented voice would boom across the waves:

"Ve vere robbed;" or "It vas nedder a penalty."

This became somewhat of an irritation to the local people and they not unreasonably began to complain to the council.

The council held a meeting to discuss the problem and see if they could find a way to stop the duke from shouting rude things at the local taxpayers.

They looked in the large book of things that the council owned and were dismayed to find that they owned neither a battleship nor a submarine with which they could sink the duke's yacht. In fact the only maritime craft that they owned was a small pleasure boat called "The Saucy Sue" that took holiday makers for trips around the harbour.

During the course of the meeting, it was also pointed out by the municipal treasurer that not only was it a dubious penalty decision in the first place, but should the council be seen to use force, it could be construed as an act of war. The cost of which was something that had not been allowed for within the current budget. A way had to be found to get rid of the duke without it appearing that the council had a hand in doing so. They would have to find an outside agency to help them.

So it was that the town secretary trawled through the files to see if there was an independent navy or some assassins listed within the local area. Unfortunately despite looking three times, she found that there were none. But what she did find was the phone number of Britain's last pirate.

His name was Colin Loppy and he worked for the local bank. When he had first joined straight from school, there had been no indication of his pirate leanings. He had appeared to be just another junior bank worker. But as the years went on, he began to slowly change his appearance. It started by the wearing of frilly shirts, and then progressed to ear-rings, sea-boots, tri-cornered hats, a moustache and an eye patch. When he started to arrive at work with a parrot stapled to his shoulder, the bank felt the need to move him from the front desk away from the public and assigned him to the strongroom instead. Unfortunately, Colin had a tendency to remove the treasures from the safe deposit boxes and try to bury them in the floor. So the bank was forced put him in a back office away from everyone else and they assigned him to house insurance, where he had spent the last twenty years indexing files.

When the council approached Colin with the idea of surreptitiously employing him to remove the duke from their coastline, he was delighted to assist. He had been waiting all of his life for a moment such as this. They explained to him that the council could not be seen to be involved, but that they would leave the doors of the Saucy Sue open and the keys in the ignition and they would make sure that everyone was looking the other way when Colin "borrowed" it. His mission was simply to remove the duke and his yacht from the council boundaries.

Colin decided that he would sail out on Saturday to board the duke's yacht. The bank was closed at the weekend and he would not have to use up any of his annual holiday that way. He spent the time before the weekend in his bedroom sharpening his cutlass and practising pirate phrases and fierce looks in the mirror.

On Saturday morning he packed some sandwiches and a flask of tea and went down to the harbour to steal The Saucy Sue. A number of people had heard of his coming exploit and a large crowd had gathered on the quayside to watch him leave. A policeman had to be called to tell them to look the other way while Colin was taking the boat.

Thus it was that Colin and The Saucy Sue chugged out of the harbour to the rousing cheers of a crowd of well-wishers who could not be absolutely sure that he had left.

Despite being a pirate, Colin had never actually sailed a small boat before. There hadn't been much need for it at the house insurance section of the bank and he was unpleasantly surprised how much the little boat went up and down and side to side once he was in the open sea.

The reason pirates are called pirates is because they Arghhhhhh. And Arghhhhhh was very similar to the noise that Colin was making as he hung over the side of the boat watching his breakfast leave his body much faster than it had entered it. The constant crawling to the side of the boat made navigating the thing a more difficult task than it would normally have been and it took nearly an hour before The Saucy Sue crashed inelegantly into the side of the duke's yacht.

The duke meanwhile had been watching Colin's erratic approach with some interest, and had concluded that his fellow seafarer was in trouble. So when Colin weakly attempted to board the yacht, the duke helpfully assisted him on-board. Colin returned the favour by being violently sick on the poop deck.

He had intended to wave his cutlass about and shout, "Avast, you scurvy dog," at the duke in order to frighten him away from the territorial waters of Newhaven, but he had accidentally dropped the cutlass in the sea as he was being hauled onto the yacht and still didn't feel well enough to do more than utter a few groans.

The duke noticing that Colin's frilly shirt had traces of vomit on it, showed his uninvited guest down to the bathroom. Colin gratefully un-stapled the parrot from his shoulder, removed his jacket and shirt, and began to clean himself up. After about twenty minutes he felt a bit better and went topside to thank the duke for his help.

"Not at all," said the duke; "in many vays you were lucky to crash into me ven you did."

It transpired that Germany had realised that all of their money had been accidentally given to Liechtenstein and they had gone to the Liechtenstein National Bank and taken it all back again. The duke told Colin that he was due to weigh anchor within the hour and sail up to Hamburg in order to shout abuse at the Germans instead.

Thus it was that the scourge of Newhaven was removed from the English coast, and Colin Loppy — Britain's last pirate, returned to a hero's welcome, a large dry cleaning bill and a desk in the insurance department of the local bank.

***

A DUCK TALE

Tony Dawson had always been a keen fisherman.

Before his freak accident with the box of oranges and the grand piano that had left him with no sense of patience, he had spent most of his time quietly fishing at his local lake.

After he had been released from hospital, he had resumed his favourite pastime. He would go down to the lake and set up his rod and tackle and sit on his folding chair and wait for the fish to bite.

After five minutes, he would be drumming his fingers on his tackle box and after ten minutes, if he had not caught a fish, he would leap into the lake and try to catch one with his bare hands.

Two or three times a day, his wife would arrive carrying a set of spare clothes for him. She would tuck her dress into her knickers and wade into the water before grabbing her husband by the neck and dragging him back to dry land.

The aquatic thrashing about of a deranged fisherman sent all of the ducks that lived on the lake to the far side. This was bad news for young mothers and small children, as they could no longer feed the ducks without walking on the grass that surrounded the lake and it made their shoes dirty. So the council built a new pathway to the far side of the lake in order to reunite excitable children, bored women and hungry ducks.

Paths cost a lot of money and the council was keen to recoup its outlay. Someone suggested that if the council opened a small shop that sold bread for the ducks at the far side of the lake, the profit generated from it would pay for the cost of the path. The council thought that this was a splendid suggestion and a few weeks later, the newly built stale bread shop opened. It was an inspired idea.

Young mothers no longer had to find room in their bags to carry stale bread to the lake. The children had an abundance of out-of-date bakery items to throw at the ducks and the council was making money from its shop.

No-one had realised when the shop was being built, that there was a small glitch in the plan.

At the end of October, without notifying the council, all of the ducks launched themselves into the air and flew south for the winter.

No ducks meant no children and no children meant no bread sales. Faced with impending financial ruin, the council took radical action.

A box of rubber ducks were purchased from the local bathroom supplies warehouse. They were painted in duck colours, attached to sticks and planted in the lake close enough to the shop to encourage bread sales, but far enough into the lake to discourage close inspection.

The mothers and children returned and crusty bread rolls and wholemeal loaves were once again being hurled into the water by the children while the mothers were entertained by Mrs. Dawson wrestling her husband out of the other side of the lake.

So important was the money from the stale bread shop that when the water level dropped during a winter drought and exposed the sticks that were anchoring the ducks to the bed of the lake, the council immediately painted the ducks pink and erected a sign saying "Please feed the flamingos"

With an abundance of bread floating about in the water and a lack of genuine ducks to eat the stuff, the fish in the lake gorged themselves. The more they ate, the fatter and lazier they became. This was good news for the Dawson Family. Tony Dawson could now catch a fish simply by walking to the edge of the lake, selecting which fish he wanted and hitting it with a stout stick.

When the ducks returned in the springtime they avoided the area with the miniature pink flamingos, and as Mr. Dawson was no longer thrashing about in the near side of the lake they settled back in their original place.

People no longer had to walk all the way across to the far side to feed the ducks any-more and so didn't bother going to the shop.

The council wondered how much it would cost to move the shop to the other side of the lake.

***

AUNTIE VERA'S
INVASION OF EUROPE

Auntie Vera had always been a bit cantankerous, but people had thought that she had mellowed when she got to her eighties. She hadn't of course, it was just that no-one listened to her any-more.

Her last great bug-bear had been the European Union.

It started when the council sent a workman to her flat in her sheltered accommodation block to change her shower taps for a new set of thermostatically-controlled ones. She had asked the man why her old perfectly serviceable taps were being replaced and he informed her that it was nothing to do with him, but was a law passed by the European Parliament. She pondered over this for some time and when the following week, another man arrived to fit a smoke alarm, giving the same reason as the first one, she began to feel resentment against the policy makers. What made it worse was that every-time she accidentally left the toast under the grill and it caught fire, the wretched smoke alarm would start shrieking and she would have to turn her hearing aid off. It was all most bothersome and despite hitting the thing with a broom each morning, it still continued to work.

Auntie Vera would pass most afternoons in the day centre that was adjacent to the housing block.

She had a favourite chair near one of the radiators, and woe betides anyone who tried to lay claim to it. While drinking her tea she would moan and grumble to the care staff about all these Europeans telling her what to do.

The staff would smile and nod and ignore her.

Vera found her comrade in arms in the unlikely form of 84-year-old Kitty Gasket. Not only did Kitty listen to her, but she also agreed with her. She had been a fervent Europhobe ever since the incident in Catford in 1953 when Greek Tony had put his hand up her skirt. She would often say that if it wasn't for the reinforced gusset of her panty girdle, her life could have gone in a completely different direction.

If Auntie Vera was as loopy as a roller-coaster, Kitty Gasket was as mad as a box of frogs.

The two old ladies would pass many agreeable afternoons mulling over the disgraceful actions of the European parliament before one or the other would nod off.

The straw that broke the camel's back was when yet another council workman turned up to replace all of the light-bulbs in Auntie Vera's flat with energy saving ones. Once again it had been a European directive that had culminated in a scruffy man messing about in her home.

When Vera related the story to Kitty, she became so angry that she snapped her digestive biscuit in half.

The two ladies decided that something had to be done. It was obvious that no-one else was interested and so they would have to take matters into their own hands. Between them they decided to go to the European Parliament and give the people there a good telling off.

Kitty said that because she had spent forty years working in the stores for the Milk Marketing Board, she knew about logistics and so would arrange the travel details while Vera could spend the time thinking of what to say to everyone when they got there.

Three weeks later they were aboard a train heading for Strasbourg. Because they were both old age pensioners, they were entitled to cheap European rail travel and as the fare had not been excessive, they had enough money to pay for a hotel when they arrived at their destination.

Kitty had prepared for the journey as if it were an expedition to the source of the Nile and had packed plastic raincoats and spare handkerchiefs. She had also brought along a flask of tea and some corned beef sandwiches in case there was not any proper food on the continent. She had heard that the bread was very crusty and did not want to get it stuck under her dentures.

Upon arrival, they decided to have a quiet night in the hotel before assaulting the parliament building the next day.

The European Parliament actually takes place in two different buildings in two different countries.

For part of the year it is based in Strasbourg on the French/German border and for the rest of the time, it is based in Brussels in Belgium. It was unfortunate for Vera and Kitty that when they arrived to sort out the politicians, all of them were filling in their expense forms in a completely different country. The parliament building in Strasbourg was unoccupied save for tour guides showing small groups of visitors around.

The two old ladies, unaware that none of the power brokers were present, joined one of the tour groups. After about twenty minutes, they found themselves in the main debating chamber — the devil's lair, if you like. It was a bit of a disappointment to them that the only people present were the tour guide and half a dozen Norwegian sightseers.

Undaunted, Vera broke away from the group and mounted the speakers rostrum. She fumbled about in her bag for a while before finding her reading glasses and a piece of paper on which she had written a speech.

"Listen to me," she said, "you have all been very naughty and made a right muddle of things, so I, Vera Ackersley, and my friend Kitty Gasket, are going to take over. So from now on you will have to ask us before you try to do anything else."

She looked up and beamed. The small group of Norwegians who had not understood a word she had said gave her a polite round of applause and Kitty took a photo of her friend. Unfortunately the photograph was slightly out of focus and had most of Auntie Vera's head missing, but at least there was a record of the occasion when Europe was seized by a bloodless coup.

As they could not think of anything else to do, they visited the gift shop where Vera bought a tea-towel showing the map of Europe and Kitty bought a fridge magnet with a picture of the European flag on it. Two hours later they were back on the train heading for England.

It was during that train journey that the enormity of what they had done struck them. Looking out of the train window at the passing countryside, Kitty remarked; "Eh fancy, to think that we own all of this now." Vera had to agree that it had all gone much better than she had thought it was going to, but was concerned that they had not left the phone number of the day centre at the parliament building, so that the politicians could call them before they passed any new laws. She would have to remember to send them a letter about it when they got home.

Upon re-entering Britain, the customs official politely asked them for their passports.

"Bugger off!" said Vera. "I am the Empress of Europe."

"So am I," said Kitty.

The customs official who had already had a long day waved them through.

***

ACKNOWLEDGEMENTS

During parties I always seemed to find myself surrounded by the offspring of my friends and relatives while they attacked the drinks table and flirted with each other. While they were reducing the value of my alcohol stock I would gather the children together and make up stories. The kids enjoyed the stories and I enjoyed having a captive audience. Occasionally an adult would wander in and listen. They would often say things like "You should write that down and send it off". I would then demonstrate my abysmal grasp of what people were saying to me and ignore them.

Now many years after traumatising the first of those small children, a book of my stories exists. I'm not completely sure what sort of book it is. The nearest anyone has been able to get to it is: Children's stories for adults. Whatever it is, I hope you liked it.

It would not have been possible to produce it without the help of others, and I owe a huge debt of gratitude to my publisher Alex Brillantes of Charging Ram Books for thinking that it was worth publishing and then actually doing so. Many thanks also to Anne Warwick the producer of the splendid cartoons, a hugely talented woman with a big heart. (Contact her if you want to buy an original – she needs the money). Thanks also to Cheryl Schmidt for weeding out the thousands of typos and also thanks to my daughter Caroline who even during the dark days, always believed that it would happen.

Gary Moore

AFTERWORD

We would be delighted to hear from you, our readers, for future editions of *Churchmouse Tales*. We value your thoughts and suggestions and should you find items for correction, please do not hesitate to send us a note. Tell us which stories were particularly good and which ones didn't work for you. Most importantly, please give us feedback and if you enjoyed this *children's book for grown-ups*, let us know and please tell your family and friends. And if you feel it needs improvement, kindly let us know as well. We may even include you as a character in the next edition.

Author's website: www.chargingram.com/garymoore.html
Email the author at:
gary.moore@orange.fr

Publisher's website: www.chargingram.com
Email the publisher at:
chargingram@gmail.com

Lightning Source UK Ltd.
Milton Keynes UK
UKOW03f2336280414

230759UK00002B/387/P